The Hashish-Eater

POETRY PUBLISHED BY HIPPOCAMPUS PRESS

Eyes of the God: The Weird Fiction and Poetry of R. H. Barlow (2002)
Clark Ashton Smith, *The Last Oblivion: Best Fantastic Poems* (2003)
George Sterling, *The Thirst of Satan: Poems of Fantasy and Terror* (2003)
R. Nemo Hill, *The Strange Music of Erich Zann* (2004)
Out of the Immortal Night: Selected Works of Samuel Loveman (2004)
Sanctity and Sin: The Collected Poems and Prose Poems of Donald Wandrei (2007)
Clark Ashton Smith, *The Complete Poetry and Translations* (in three volumes; 2007–8)

Clark Ashton Smith

The Hashish-Eater

Edited, with notes, &c., by Donald Sidney-Fryer

Hippocampus Press

New York

This compilation is copyright © 2008 by Donald Sidney-Fryer.

Cordial acknowledgement is made to CASiana Literary Enterprises and Arkham House for permission to use materials by Clark Ashton Smith. The publisher also wishes to thank Terence McVicker, Dwayne Olson, Philip J. Rahman, and Scott Connors for their assistance.

Previous publication data:
   The Hashish-Eater, published in Smith, *Ebony and Crystal* (Auburn Journal, 1922); in August Derleth (editor), *Dark of the Moon* (Arkham House), 1947; in Smith, *Selected Poems* (Arkham House, 1971); as a separate booklet (Necronomicon Press, 1989). The text here is based on the versions in *Ebony and Crystal* and *Selected Poems.*
   "The Crystals," included in Smith, *Poems in Prose* (Arkham House, 1965); in Smith, *Nostalgia of the Unknown: The Complete Prose Poetry* (Necronomicon Press, 1988).
   "Argument of *The Hashish-Eater,*" included in Smith, *Strange Shadows* (Greenwood Press, 1989).
   "The Face from Infinity," included in *The Black Book of Clark Ashton Smith* (Arkham House, 1979).
   Letter from Smith to S. J. Sackett, dated 11 July 1950, included in Donald Sidney-Fryer (compiler), *Emperor of Dreams: A Clark Ashton Smith Bibliography* (Donald M. Grant, 1978).

The compiler and author of this booklet gratefully acknowledges the special assistance, interest, and support of Ronald S. Hilger, Grass Valley, California; Henry J. Vester III, Klamath Falls, Oregon; and David E. Schultz.

Copyright © 2008 by Hippocampus Press

Published by Hippocampus Press
P.O. Box 641, New York, NY 10156.
http://www.hippocampuspress.com

Cover illustration by Clark Ashton Smith for "The Hashish-Eater." Cover design by Barbara Briggs Silbert.
Hippocampus Press logo designed by Anastasia Damianakos.

1 3 5 7 9 8 6 4 2

ISBN13: 978-0-9793806-8-6

CONTENTS

A Wind from the Unknown

Who of us care to be present at the *accouchement* of the immortal? I think that we so attend who are first to take this book in our hands. A bold assertion, truly, and one demonstrable only in years remote from these; and—dust wages no war with dust. But it is one of those things that I should most "like to come back and see."

With these words in 1922, George Sterling opened his preface to *Ebony and Crystal,* perhaps the greatest collection of original poems ever produced by his young friend and protégé Clark Ashton Smith, and containing as its centerpiece what many consider Smith's finest poetic achievement, "The Hashish-Eater." At nearly 600 lines, this is not only Smith's longest poem but also his most characteristically *Smithian,* and might well be described as an epic journey through the endless universe of the human imagination.

If Sterling were somehow granted his wish to "come back and see," what might he learn regarding the estimation of Clark Ashton Smith during the opening years of the twenty-first century? Smith's poetry unfortunately has not received the widespread recognition and appreciation it so richly deserves; on the other hand, his fiction is being increasingly reprinted and is gaining the attention of an ever-widening audience. This favorable recognition is due in large part to Smith's own protégé Donald Sidney-Fryer, whose tireless efforts on behalf of the Romantic tradition of poetry in general, and of Clark Ashton Smith in particular, has spanned more than forty-five years. During this period Sidney-Fryer has edited or written more than a dozen books or pamphlets by or about Ashton Smith and has written many essays on Smith, as well as on Ambrose Bierce, Robert E. Howard, George Sterling, and Nora May French among others. Aside from these scholarly pursuits, Sidney-Fryer has performed dramatic readings from *The Faerie Queene* and other poems in countless venues, both in the U.S. and abroad, and is himself an accomplished poet with three published collections of his own finely crafted poetry.

All this accumulated knowledge and expertise combined with his unique talents as both poet and performer qualify Donald Sidney-Fryer as the perfect person not only to bring Smith's most famous poem to a wider audience, but also to present it in a form more "user friendly" to the general reading public; and if ever there was a poem worthy of explanation and annotation, this is it! Indeed, Smith's daunting vocabulary is one of the main reasons "The Hashish-Eater" is not more widely appreciated. Smith delighted in archaic and unusual words, and has filled this poem with such words as "Hecatompylos" and "Saiph" among many other references to Greek, Egyptian, Arabic and Hebrew mythologies. For this reason the glossary of unusual words is an indispensable tool for the comprehensive enjoyment of this poem, and it is strongly suggested that the reader consult this glossary as necessary.

Another important benefit of the audio performance included here is the simple ability to listen to the poem spoken both properly and dramatically in conjunction with reading the text, thus enhancing the experience both aesthetically and intellectually. As Sidney-Fryer points out in his fine introduction to the Timescape paperback *The Last Incantation,* "Like any self-respecting veteran poet, Clark was long accustomed to the habit and necessity of reading his own poetry aloud and of literally testing its interior and exterior sonics . . . this testing of the poetry's music and magic, by declaiming it over and over again (whether aloud or within the 'inner ear' of the poet) formed, perhaps, the most crucial part of the poetic process." Smith *designed* his poetry to be spoken and heard aloud; so in this aesthetic sense, here is Clark Ashton Smith's poetic masterpiece as he intended it to be experienced!

Not only will the lover of poetry benefit from a close study of this remarkable poem, but likewise the aficionado of CAS's fiction will find many glimpses into the fantastic realms of Smith's later fiction. "The Hashish-Eater" serves as a veritable well-spring of ideas and inspiration later developed into his better known weird tales. For example: lines 192–96 state "For the snows / Of hyperborean winter, and their winds, / sleep in his jewel-builded capital, / Nor any charm of flame-wrought wizardry, / Nor conjured suns may rout them; so he flees," an obvious precursor of the Hyperborean series and to "The Coming of the White Worm" in particular. In fact, Lovecraft himself could possibly have found inspiration for his great Old Ones (Cthulhu in particular) in such lines as "Bulks of enormous crimson, kraken-limbed / And kraken-headed, lifting up as crowns / The octiremes of perished emperors."

In closing, let us return once more to the words of George Sterling which remain as pertinent, fresh, and eloquent as when they were penned more than eighty years ago.

—RON HILGER
Grass Valley, California

Because he has lent himself the more innocently to the whispers of his subconscious daemon, and because he has set those murmurs to purer and harder crystal than we others, by so much the longer will the poems of Clark Ashton Smith endure. Here indeed is loot against the forays of moth and rust. Here we shall find none or little of the sentimental fat with which so much of our literature is larded. Rather shall one in Imagination's "misty mid-region," see elfin rubies burn at his feet, witch-fires glow in the nearer cypresses, and feel upon his brow a wind from the unknown. The brave hunters of fly-specks on Art's cathedral windows will find little here for their trouble, and both the stupid and the over-sophisticated had best stare owlishly and pass by: here are neither kindergartens nor skyscrapers. But let him who is worthy by reason of his clear eye and unjaded heart wander across these borders of beauty and mystery and be glad.

—GEORGE STERLING.
San Francisco, October 28, 1922.

About Clark Ashton Smith and *The Hashish-Eater*

The Californian poet and writer of fantastic stories Clark Ashton Smith was born on 13 January 1893 in Long Valley and died on 14 August 1961 at Pacific Grove on the Monterey Peninsula, where he had moved after his marriage to Carol Jones Dorman in late 1954. Otherwise, he lived most of his life in a three-room cabin built by his parents, Timeus Smith and Mary Francis Gaylord Smith, called Fanny, on Boulder or Indian Ridge some few miles south or southeast of the old historical part of Auburn. Smith sold most of their land in late 1937 and early 1938, after his mother's death in mid-1935 and his father's death in late 1937. The few acres still left from the sale of the original forty acres became surrounded by modern residential developments. Clark Ashton Smith is survived by three stepchildren.

Smith began writing prose at the age of eleven; these were imitations of European fairy tales and that huge collection of Arabian folklore, fable, and mythology, *The Thousand and One Nights*, otherwise known as *The Arabian Nights*, a work that fascinated and enchanted his childhood and adolescence, and obviously influenced his literary output throughout his lifetime. At the age of thirteen he discovered the poetry and prose of Edgar Allan Poe and began writing his first verse at that same age. Smith had his first prose fictions published in 1910, 1911, and 1912 in the *Overland Monthly* and the *Black Cat*. In early 1911 he began corresponding with George Sterling, then the unofficial poet laureate of California, and accounted at that time the great poet of the West Coast. Sterling's two greatest poems, *The Testimony of the Suns* and "A Wine of Wizardry," were first published in book form in 1903 and 1909, respectively, and exercised a profound influence on the young Smith. The correspondence and friendship between Smith and Sterling lasted until November 1926 when the elder poet died. Smith became a protégé and a kind of pupil to Sterling, who did everything in his power to help and encourage him, and to propagandize on behalf of his poetry. Smith's early, persistent, and copious experiments in verse led to his first mature poetry, created during 1911–12, and resulted in his first major collection *The Star-Treader*, published in late 1912.

In addition to *The Star-Treader*, Smith published two other major collections during his early poetic career. These were *Ebony and Crystal*, appearing in late 1922, and *Sandalwood*, in late 1925. In mid-1918, the distinguished and prestigious Book Club of California, based in San Francisco, published a small but elegantly printed selection of Smith's poems under the title *Odes and Sonnets*. Smith and Sterling were evidently among the few Californian poets thus honored with collections published by this organization, which has usually specialized in monographs on subjects in Californian history and culture. Smith's early poetic career lasted from 1911 on into the later 1920s. His principal career as a fictioneer lasted from the late 1920s into the later 1930s. However, from the late 1930s until his death he became once again primarily a poet. It should be stated that, by the early to middle 1920s, Smith had become widely known as a lyric poet of exceptional distinction, and that his early collections of poetry in general received extraordinary praise, not only from the literary critics in San Francisco but also, and just as much, from a broad spectrum of littérateurs in the U.S. and in Great Britain. He had thus already achieved a solid reputation years before he began writing the fantastic stories typical of his literary maturity and having them published in a wide variety of pulp magazines during the 1930s, the Golden Age of such periodicals.

Persons unacquainted with Smith and his art, but who would like to learn more about his life and variegated career as imaginative writer, poet, artist, and sculptor, are urged to visit the California Section in the State Library located in the Library/Courts Building II immediately southwest of the old Capitol building in downtown Sacramento. The State Library possesses most of the book and booklet publications with material written by him as well as most of the books about him and his various arts.

Although still not widely known to a general or mass audience, Clark Ashton Smith has always had the esteem and considerable admiration of connoisseurs, and moreover has had them since the start of his mature literary career during 1911–12. He is undoubtedly one of the greatest practitioners of the fantastic fable—he is at least on a par with the late great Jorge Luis Borges—and certainly he ranks as a great poet, and one of the most original of the twentieth century. His vision and style are at once luxuriant and compact, often otherworldly in subject matter, and together with his pursuit of truth, his philosophy is austere, unflinching, and uncompromising. As an example of the austerity of his thought, we have the following apothegm: "All human thought, all science, all religion, is the holding of a candle to the night of the universe." Another apothegm, this time in regard to the general or primordial darkness in the midst of which exist both our own planet and the cosmos at large: "Because science has lit a few artificial lights amid the darkness of things, modern man tends to forget that the darkness still exists."

Smith possesses unusual depth, perception, and wisdom. He is probably unique in having, within the body of any literature in any language anywhere, the most highly developed sense of cosmic consciousness, or of cosmic-astronomic consciousness, possibly even greater than the same in the output of Edmund Spenser, John Milton, George Sterling, and H. P. Lovecraft. Smith also has one of the largest vocabularies of any author in any language, a vocabulary moreover that he uses with particular depth, color, and precision. Those rare individuals who can revel in the challenge, richness, fascination, and apparent unlimitedness of the English language, its utter lexicographical magnificence, will find in Smith's oeuvre a choice and unparalleled feast of words. *The Hashish-Eater* furnishes us with a perfect example of Smith's cosmic-astronomic sense, his especial type of fantastic fable, as well as his often singularly choice vocabulary. Hashish is used in this poem only as a symbol of exaltation and expansion; Smith certainly had not taken any hashish by the time he created the poem, although apparently he did experiment with drugs sometime in the latter part of his life, in addition to being an evidently lifelong devotee of assorted hard spirits and Californian wines, but rarely to excess.

Whereas *Sandalwood* was the product of the first half of the 1920s, Smith created the poems included in *Ebony and Crystal* primarily during the years 1913 to 1918. He gathered the poems, and structured the collection, during 1918 and 1919. Although a hugely gifted and inspired poet, he was nonetheless a careful technician and a fastidious craftsman, rarely leaving anything to chance or carelessness. The one extraordinary exception to this is his longest and greatest poem, totaling almost

600 lines, *The Hashish-Eater*, which he created in early 1920, apparently after he had already completed the manuscript of *Ebony and Crystal*. He had blocked out the poem's first 50 lines more or less by mid-January. According to his later testimony, he roughed out the first draft, in an overall accounting, in some 10 or 12 days, averaging about 50 lines per day. By the end of January alone, he had achieved about 300 lines, and sometime after mid-February he must have completed at least the first draft, since the date of completion of composition is given as 20 February 1920. To have completed such a work in a month or a little more overall must be accounted an extraordinary accomplishment—if not even stupefying—in terms of the sustained white-hot quality of its otherworldly imagery and invention. Considering such imagination as is displayed in this poem, nobody could have written it in that amount of time while also making a special diet of hashish!

Compared to his usual deliberate method of poetic productivity, *The Hashish-Eater* came virtually boiling or seething up from his subconscious, insistently dictating itself to his conscious mind. Rather than holding out for separate publication, as he might well have done, Smith instead opted to include this colossal poem, this compressed or compact epic, as the more or less central selection in *Ebony and Crystal*. Technically the work is amazing, inasmuch as there is hardly a single device of epic or lyric poetry, apart from rime, that he does not employ, choosing to cast it in an especially exhilarating type of blank verse, with a noticeably insistent beat, and creating thereby a new type of poetic music that, as particularly achieved in blank verse in English, seems to subsume within it every other previous type from the Elizabethans onward, through John Milton and up through the poetic masters of the nineteenth century, Smith's immediate poetic predecessors. It is very much the product of someone who, in addition to the extraordinary resources afforded by his own imagination, vision, and invention, has profoundly studied and thoroughly assimilated Sterling's own two greatest works, *The Testimony of the Suns* and "A Wine of Wizardry." Although it stands in the immediate tradition of "A Wine of Wizardry," it is not *per se* a direct imitation of that older poem.

Not surprisingly, in terms of subject or theme, vocabulary, and general direction and style, Smith's massive poem sums up all his other mature poetry created from 1911 up into early 1920, and gathered into *The Star-Treader* and *Ebony and Crystal* both. Although a product of the first half of the 1920s, *Sandalwood* continues the same general direction and style of his first two major collections, but is itself primarily a collection of love poems, and thus is more immediately personal in tone and perhaps more forthrightly human and accessible than the other two. Whereas they are more epic and ambitious in scope, *Sandalwood* is more intimate but no less finely wrought. However, if on the one hand *The Hashish-Eater* may serve more or less in general terms as a convenient index to the output of his early poetic career from 1911 to the later 1920s, on the other hand the same compressed epic may serve in subject, style, and vocabulary as an equally convenient index to the adult prose fictions that he was to create from the late 1920s to the late 1930s. His best prose fictions often take place in other worlds deliberately created by the author but often derived from subtle hints found in obscure corners of older mythologies, legendry, and folklore, whether of the Orient or of the Occident. During the 1930s Smith became an early writer of unusually distinctive and literate science fiction or science fantasy among other types of fiction, in which he often continues the themes and subjects first essayed in *The Star-Treader* of 1912.

His best and most characteristic stories are fantasies that could be termed more or less accurately as parables, fables, or allegories of emotional, psychological, and spiritual (i.e., non-material) truth, as well as of cosmic wisdom. As only one example of the striking continuity from his early poems on into his later fiction, the following episode may be cited from lines 65–72 of *The Hashish-Eater*:

> And I see,
> In gardens of a crimson-litten world,
> The sacred flow'r with lips of purple flesh,
> And silver-lashed, vermillion-lidded eyes
> Of torpid azure; whom his furtive priests
> At moonless eve in terror seek to slay,
> With bubbling grails of sacrificial blood
> That hide a hueless poison.

Smith later developed the same subject that very same year, sometime during the summer or early autumn, in his prose-poem "The Flower-Devil," which he expanded, later still, during October 1931, into the short story "The Demon of the Flower."

It should be mentioned in passing that at the very least Smith is, in terms of the English language, the foremost creator within the genre of the poem in prose. This genre is not to be confused with modern poetry in general, which is often or usually written in prose in lines of varying length with or without a noticeable metre or stress. In his prose-poems Smith follows immediately in the wake or footsteps of those French poets mostly of the nineteenth century, who created the form or medium of the *poème en prose*, and those others who then worked extensively within it. Smith's complete prose-poems have now been collected several times in book or booklet form.

In addition to *The Thousand and One Nights*, there are a number of other obvious elements and sources involved in the creation or background of *The Hashish-Eater*, elements and sources deserving of separate mention, in particular the vocabulary used and how the poet came to acquire it. Smith was extremely well read and knowledgeable in all manner of disciplines and subjects, especially languages, history, mythology, astronomy, and geology, among many others. His higher education was largely a matter of self-instruction. He had more or less attended grammar school, first in Long Valley and then in Auburn, whenever his long bouts of childhood illness had permitted him to do so. After he had attended for only a few days or so the old Placer Union High School (now replaced by another building) located in Auburn, he together with his parents decided that he himself could take better charge of his own education; and so he stayed at home, and put himself through an exceptional program of educational discipline during his early through middle teens. This program included his going through the entire *Webster's Unabridged Dictionary*, page by page and word by word, studying not only the various literal and secondary or derived meanings of all the words but also their etymologies, taking this aspect of his linguistic studies in most or many cases as far back as he could to their origins in Sanskrit. The dictionary just mentioned was possibly the edition published in 1909, i.e., the very first one of *Webster's New International Dictionary*. It should be mentioned in passing that Smith later taught himself at least Latin, French, and Spanish, not only in order to read their various literatures— expending considerable time and energy in translating from the works of poets who have written in French or Spanish—but also well enough in

French and Spanish to be able to create perfectly decent original poems in those languages.

When we state, for example, that among other things, he studied astronomy and geology, this is not meant just in an abstract sense, i.e., out of books. Books he used, indeed, and apparently all the time. However, in addition, he would have studied the heavens visible from his home outside Auburn with the aid of star charts, becoming extremely familiar with both the nearby and the more remote stars and constellations. This is evident throughout his output, but especially in *The Hashish-Eater* as well as in his first major volume of poems, *The Star-Treader*. We must not forget that, at the time of his childhood, adolescence, and young adulthood, the state capital of Sacramento was a much smaller city, and Smith's own Auburn was likewise a much smaller town. The sheer physical perception of the nocturnal heavens possible at that time did not have as barrier or obstacle "the hell-bright lamps of cities," as he termed them in one of his very last poems. Similarly he would have known geology not only from textbooks or manuals but, at least equally so, from his own careful observations of the terrain immediately around his home, including the abandoned gold and other mines that came into operation from the time of the Gold Rush on into the latter half of the nineteenth century.

Among other elements appearing in *The Hashish-Eater*, there must be mentioned the quite overt presence of demons and implicit demonologies, not only as developed in mediaeval Europe (largely deriving, oddly enough, from Plato's philosophical writings), but just as much throughout Hindu India, the early far-flung Arab world, and the Buddhism originating in India and spreading into Burma, Thailand, Cambodia, Vietnam, Malaysia, Indonesia, Tibet, China, Korea, Japan, and elsewhere.

Let us continue with our list of important odds and ends in Smith's poem deserving of separate notice. When Smith mentions some flora or fauna or what-have-you as being in some star, this means, of course, in some world or planet orbiting around that star or in some constellation identified by the same star. The poem's first section, or verse paragraph, describes the supreme ascendance of the poet, the visionary, the dreamer, the Hashish-Eater, or the Man-God, to use a term and concept developed by the French poet Charles Pierre Baudelaire, a writer greatly admired by Smith, and from whose principal collection of poetry *Les Fleurs du mal* (*The Flowers of Ill*) he was to translate during the 1920s. To image the poem's first section properly—and to get a feeling for the sense of power and expansion intended—one should think of an extralarge Cinemascope or Cinerama screen virtually surrounding one and exhibiting something comparable to a NASA rocket taking off at Cape Canaveral, Florida!

Soon after the start of the second section, the poet states: "I convoke / The Babel of their visions [i.e., the evidence of the "senses multitudinous"], and attend / At once their myriad witness:" This effect would be somewhat analogous—and this is the closest analogy that comes readily to mind—to certain scenes in the science-fiction film *The Man Who Fell to Earth* (starring David Bowie), scenes wherein the hero has whole banks of TV sets turned on, one bank above another, and is looking at all of them more or less at the same time, or as much as he can assimilate.

The Hashish-Eater, the hero of Smith's compressed epic, is the same as that Man-God who is described by Baudelaire in his monograph *Les Paradis artificiels* (*Artificial Paradises*), published in 1861. We should mention that the French poet himself often partook liberally of alcohol, opium, and hashish, and knew precisely what he was describing. In this work, partially translating from Thomas De Quincey's *Confessions of an English Opium-Eater* (1812), Baudelaire develops the concept of *l'Homme-Dieu*, or the Man-God, who—upon partaking of mind- or mood-altering drugs, whether by eating or smoking—undergoes such a feeling of exaltation that he experiences himself not merely to be *one with* God but to *be* God. Of course, the one and often overwhelming disadvantage of the drug-induced state is that it can enhance not only the pleasurable feelings and moods but the non-pleasurable ones as well! If the drug-partaker loses his balance or control, or if something external to him should happen so that the exaltation and euphoria are changed into feelings of genuine fright, horror, terror, and paranoia, then he runs the risk of undergoing an awful, gut-wrenching experience of the most depressing kind, and so he must beware of this negative potential as well.

Later in Smith's poem, when the dreamer can mingle with his visions, he is "in a state similar to the Buddhic plane," according to the poet writing elsewhere. The Buddhic plane is defined as the fifth dimension, the level of consciousness where the oneness of all life becomes apparent, and where ascension begins; thus Buddhic substance based in unconditional love. Apparently it is a state attained through contemplation or meditation, a state wherefrom one can perceive and experience the interpenetration and identification of all things in the universal consciousness. Furthermore, it seems to be a state wherefrom the adept can perceive, as in a state of cosmic consciousness, the various lives and conditions implicit in the various dimensions of life, dream, and thought (these last terms are used in this immediate context as being alike in significance). And with these various lives and conditions, the adept may or may not identify in the manner of a god who is both present and yet apart.

Throughout the narrative of Smith's poem, but especially at its very end with the final image, the "huge white eyeless Face, / That fills the void and fills the universe, / And bloats against the limits of the world / With lips of flame that open," the concept of the Demiurge is implicitly and explicitly invoked. In Platonic philosophy, the Demiurge is the subordinate god, not the supreme one, who has created the world or universe, i.e., the cosmos. In some Gnostic systems, he is an inferior god, not absolutely intelligent, but nonetheless the creator of the world, identified by some with the creator God of the Old Testament, and carefully distinguished from the supreme God.

This brings us to the phenomenon of Gnosticism, one of the most fascinating developments of the ancient Mediterranean world and of the ancient Near or Middle East. This was a philosophical and religious movement of pre-Christian times as well as of later with several forms, both Christian and non-Christian, all of which were characterized by the central doctrine that emancipation comes through knowledge, i.e., the gnosis, the possession of which saves the initiates from the clutch of matter or of the material world. Gnosis is thus positive knowledge, especially spiritual truth, as claimed by the Gnostics.

The central doctrine of Gnosticism is rather similar to that of non-attachment to the material world—and thus to delusion, hatred, and passion—as practiced by many denominations of the Hindu and Buddhist religions. By the practice of this doctrine of non-attachment, the adept or initiate may attain that state or condition whereby he may be released from the unending chain of matter, of physical being, and thus from the necessity of future incarnations, a state or condition whereby one may pass into nirvana, or nothingness, when and where one's own personal identity is lost in the Whole, the One, the Absolute, or God.

There is a rather curious paradox involved in all this thinking, theory, or conjecture. If on the one hand God has created the cosmos and endowed all sentient things with life and energy—and has become thereby released from the awful tedium of infinity and of nothingness as well as from the equally awful contemplation thereof—on the other hand, throughout that same infinity or eternity, all the entities thus endowed by God with life, and especially with self-consciousness, seemingly yearn in some form or fashion to return to their source, and thus to lose themselves in that Whole, that One, that Absolute.

There are many things that could be stated in admiring comment of Smith's poem as an artistic construct, but one extremely pertinent and creative point is that made by a contemporary admirer of this poet. As pointed out by Henry J. Vester III, a distinguished aficionado of modern imaginative literature, one of the most impressive aspects of Smith's work, whether in prose or in poetry, but possibly nowhere more evident than in *The Hashish-Eater*, is the sustained and yet carefully modulated excitement that so subtly communicates such tremendous depths of passion, whether it be the passion of wonder, of ecstasy, or of overwhelming terror. Even despair and pathos have their peculiar and variegated passions in the output of this poet, just as they do, perhaps much more commonly, in music.

The text of *The Hashish-Eater* used is the original as published in *Ebony and Crystal* (December 1922), appearing here on the verso pages, and the somewhat revised version (c. 1945–49) published in *Selected Poems* (1971), appearing here on the recto pages.

Much of the data contained in the preceding account of Smith's life and career, and of *The Hashish-Eater*, is taken from *Emperor of Dreams: A Clark Ashton Smith Bibliography*, compiled by Donald Sidney-Fryer (West Kingston, RI: Donald M. Grant, 1978), from Smith's letters to George Sterling (their entire correspondence, together with related papers and artwork, is now part of the New York Public Library's Berg Collection; the letters are published in *The Shadow of the Unattained: The Letters of George Sterling and Clark Ashton Smith*, edited by David E. Schultz and S. T. Joshi [New York: Hippocampus Press, 2005]), or from essays, whether published or as yet unpublished, written by the bibliography's compiler.

The Crystals

Raptly as one who would divine the perilous eyes of Sleep, and the dreams and mysteries which lurk therein, I sought to fathom the gulf-enclosing orb of the crystal: Void for a time, and hollow with light it was, and transpicuous like the orient sky that is made clear for the colours of the dawn. But soon the light was centered to a star, and the crystal itself, as if pregnant with the Infinite, became a tenebrous and profound abysm, through which a teeming myriad of shadows, vague as incipient dreams, or luminous with a glimpse of vision not prefigurable, fled in an ever-changing phantasmagoric succession about the star:

From out those vortical and swirling glooms, where only the central star was constant, I saw the pallor of innominable faces emerge—faces that broke like bubbles; and forms that were strange as conceptions of an alien sun, with the eidolons of things which were imageless before, swam for a little in that phantasmic wave. But all the multifold mysteries which were manifest therein, I knew for the hidden thoughts and occluse, reluctant dreams of mine under-soul—thoughts and dreams now shadow-shown in the gulf-revealing orb of the hollow crystal. . . .

Thus, in the crystal of Time and Space, whose gulfs contain all that we call the Infinite, may God behold the manifestation of all the multiform mysteries, and all the secret thoughts and dreams which abide in the centremost sanctuary of His Being. And naught may appear to Him but these—His thoughts and dreams forever shadow-shown in the immeasurable orb of the hollow crystal of Time and Space.

[The poem in prose above was written on 27 July 1914.]

Argument of *The Hashish-Eater*

By some exaltation and expansion of cosmic consciousness, rather than a mere drug, used here as a symbol, the dreamer is carried to a height from which he beholds the strange and multiform scenes of existence in alien worlds; he maintains control of his visions, evokes and dismisses them at will. Then, in a state similar to the Buddhic plane, he is able to mingle with them and identify himself with their actors and objects. Still later, there is a transition in which the visions, and the monstrous and demonic forces he has evoked, begin to overpower him, to hurry him on helplessly, under circumstances of fright and panic. Armies of fiends and monsters, many drawn from the worlds of myth and fable, muster against him, pursue him through a terrible cosmos, and he is driven at last to the verge of a gulf into which fall in cataracts the ruin and rubble of the universe; a gulf from which the face of infinity itself, in all its awful blankness, beyond stars and worlds, beyond created things, even fiends and monsters, rises up to confront him.

[The abstract or summary above was evidently written sometime after the creation of the poem itself. As extant, it is incomplete.]

The poem's last lines and final image:

The Face of Infinity

I see a tiny star within the depths —
A light that stays me, while the wings of doom
Convene their thickening thousands: For the star
Increases, taking to its hueless orb,
With all the speed of horror-changèd dreams,
The light as of a million million moons:
And floating up through gulfs and glooms eclipsed,
It grows and grows, a huge white eyeless Face,
That fills the void and fills the universe,
And bloats against the limits of the world
With lips of flame that open. ****

[The above is taken from the poem's final section, lines 566–76.]

The Face from Infinity

A man who fears the sky for some indefinable reason, and tries to avoid the open as much as possible. Dying at last in a room with short, curtained windows, he finds himself suddenly on a vast, bare plain beneath a void heaven. Into this heaven, slowly, there arises a dreadful, infinite face, from which he can find no refuge, since all his senses have apparently been

22

merged in the one sense of sight. Death, for him, is the eternal moment in which he confronts the face, and knows why he has always feared the sky.

[The plot-germ or plot-sketch above is taken from *The Black Book of Clark Ashton Smith*, the author's commonplace book, i.e., his notebook, in use from about 1929 to 1961, where the plot-germ figures as item no. 4.]

Excerpt from a letter by Smith, summer 1950

[During the summer of 1950, in response to an inquiry about the elaborate style characteristic of much of his prose and poetry, Smith wrote in part as follows, in his letter dated 11 July 1950, to S. J. Sackett, a professor of English at the state college in Hays, Kansas. The text, quoted in full, contains an important and enlightening statement in explanation of the author's intent, formulated thus *a posteriori*, in creating *The Hashish-Eater*.]

As to coinages [i.e., coined words], I have really made few such, apart from proper names of personages, cities, countries, deities, etc., in realms lying "east of the sun and west of the moon." I have used a few words, names of fabulous monsters, etc., drawn from Herodotus, [Sir John] Maundeville, and Flaubert, which I have not been able to find in dictionaries or other works of reference. Some of these occur in *The Hashish-Eater*, a much misunderstood poem, which was intended as a study in cosmic consciousness, drawing heavily on myth and fable for its imagery.

It is my own theory that, if the infinite worlds of the cosmos were opened to human vision, the visionary would be overwhelmed by horror in the end, like the hero of this poem.

["Herodotus, Maundeville, and Flaubert": The references here are to the *Histories* of Herodotus, *The Voyages and Travels of Sir John Maundeville* (in contemporary usage as *Mandeville*), and *La Tentation de Saint Antoine* (*The Temptation of Saint Anthony*) by Gustave Flaubert, as extant in Lafcadio Hearn's English translation.]

The Hashish-Eater;
or, The Apocalypse of Evil

Bow down: I am the emperor of dreams;
I crown me with the million-coloured sun
Of secret worlds incredible, and take
Their trailing skies for vestment, when I soar,
Throned on the mounting zenith, and illume   5
The spaceward-flown horizons infinite.
Like rampant monsters roaring for their glut,
The fiery-crested oceans rise and rise,
By jealous moons maleficently urged
To follow me forever; mountains horned   10
With peaks of sharpest adamant, and mawed
With sulphur-lit volcanoes lava-langued,
Usurp the skies with thunder, but in vain;
And continents of serpent-shapen trees,
With slimy trunks that lengthen league by league,   15
Pursue my flight through ages spurned to fire
By that supreme ascendance. Sorcerers,
And evil kings predominantly armed
With scrolls of fulvous dragon-skin, whereon
Are worm-like runes of ever-twisting flame,   20
Would stay me; and the sirens of the stars,
With foam-light songs from silver fragrance wrought,
Would lure me to their crystal reefs; and moons
Where viper-eyed, senescent devils dwell,
With antic gnomes abominably wise,   25
Heave up their icy horns across my way:
But naught deters me from the goal ordained
By suns, and aeons, and immortal wars,

Bow down: I am the emperor of dreams;
I crown me with the million-colored sun
Of secret worlds incredible, and take
Their trailing skies for vestment when I soar,
Throned on the mounting zenith, and illume   5
The spaceward-flown horizon infinite.
Like rampant monsters roaring for their glut,
The fiery-crested oceans rise and rise,
By jealous moons maleficently urged
To follow me for ever; mountains horned   10
With peaks of sharpest adamant, and mawed
With sulphur-lit volcanoes lava-langued,
Usurp the skies with thunder, but in vain;
And continents of serpent-shapen trees,
With slimy trunks that lengthen league by league,   15
Pursue my flight through ages spurned to fire
By that supreme ascendance; sorcerers,
And evil kings, predominantly armed
With scrolls of fulvous dragon-skin whereon
Are worm-like runes of ever-twisting flame,   20
Would stay me; and the sirens of the stars,
With foam-like songs from silver fragrance wrought,
Would lure me to their crystal reefs; and moons
Where viper-eyed, senescent devils dwell,
With antic gnomes abominably wise,   25
Heave up their icy horns across my way.
But naught deters me from the goal ordained
By suns and eons and immortal wars,

27

And sung by moons and motes; the goal whose name
Is all the secret of forgotten glyphs,   30
By sinful gods in torrid rubies writ
For ending of a brazen book; the goal
Whereat my soaring ecstasy may stand,
In amplest heavens multiplied to hold
My hordes of thunder-vested avatars,   35
And Promethèan armies of my thought,
That brandish claspèd levins. There I call
My memories, intolerably clad
In light the peaks of paradise may wear,
And lead the Armageddon of my dreams,   40
Whose instant shout of triumph is become
Immensity's own music: For their feet
Are founded on innumerable worlds,
Remote in alien epochs, and their arms
Upraised, are columns potent to exalt   45
With ease ineffable the countless thrones
Of all the gods that are and gods to be,
Or bear the seats of Asmadai and Set
Above the seventh paradise.

                                     Supreme
In culminant omniscience manifold,   50
And served by senses multitudinous,
Far-posted on the shifting walls of time,
With eyes that roam the star-unwinnowed fields
Of utter night and chaos, I convoke

And sung by moons and motes; the goal whose name
Is all the secret of forgotten glyphs   30
By sinful gods in torrid rubies writ
For ending of a brazen book; the goal
Whereat my soaring ecstasy may stand
In amplest heavens multiplied to hold
My hordes of thunder-vested avatars,   35
And Promethèan armies of my thought,
That brandish claspèd levins. There I call
My memories, intolerably clad
In light the peaks of paradise may wear,
And lead the Armageddon of my dreams   40
Whose instant shout of triumph is become
Immensity's own music: for their feet
Are founded on innumerable worlds,
Remote in alien epochs, and their arms
Upraised, are columns potent to exalt   45
With ease ineffable the countless thrones
Of all the gods that are or gods to be,
And bear the seats of Asmodai and Set
Above the seventh paradise.

                              Supreme
In culminant omniscience manifold,   50
And served by senses multitudinous,
Far-posted on the shifting walls of time,
With eyes that roam the star-unwinnowed fields
Of utter night and chaos, I convoke

The Babel of their visions, and attend   55
At once their myriad witness: I behold,
In Ombos, where the fallen Titans dwell,
With mountain-builded walls, and gulfs for moat,
The secret cleft that cunning dwarves have dug
Beneath an alp-like buttress; and I list,   60
Too late, the clang of adamantine gongs,
Dinned by their drowsy guardians, whose feet
Have felt the wasp-like sting of little knives,
Embrued with slobber of the basilisk,
Or juice of wounded upas. And I see,   65
In gardens of a crimson-litten world,
The sacred flow'r with lips of purple flesh,
And silver-lashed, vermilion-lidded eyes
Of torpid azure; whom his furtive priests
At moonless eve in terror seek to slay,   70
With bubbling grails of sacrificial blood
That hide a hueless poison. And I read,
Upon the tongue of a forgotten sphinx,
The annuling word a spiteful demon wrote
With gall of slain chimeras; and I know   75
What pentacles the lunar wizards use,
That once allured the gulf-returning roc,
With ten great wings of furlèd storm, to pause
Midmost an alabaster mount; and there,
With boulder-weighted webs of dragons'-gut,   80
Uplift by cranes a captive giant built,
They wound the monstrous, moonquake-throbbing bird,

The Babel of their visions, and attend   55
At once their myriad witness. I behold
In Ombos, where the fallen Titans dwell,
With mountain-builded walls, and gulfs for moat,
The secret cleft that cunning dwarves have dug
Beneath an alp-like buttress; and I list,   60
Too late, the clang of adamantine gongs
Dinned by their drowsy guardians, whose feet
Have felt the wasp-like sting of little knives
Embrued with slobber of the basilisk
Or the pale juice of wounded upas. In   65
Some red Antarean garden-world, I see
The sacred flower with lips of purple flesh,
And silver-lashed, vermilion-lidded eyes
Of torpid azure; whom his furtive priests
At moonless eve in terror seek to slay   70
With bubbling grails of sacrificial blood
That hide a hueless poison. And I read
Upon the tongue of a forgotten sphinx,
The annulling word a spiteful demon wrote
In gall of slain chimeras; and I know   75
What pentacles the lunar wizards use,
That once allured the gulf-returning roc,
With ten great wings of furlèd storm, to pause
Midmost an alabaster mount; and there,
With boulder-weighted webs of dragons' gut   80
Uplift by cranes a captive giant built,
They wound the monstrous, moonquake-throbbing bird,

31

And plucked, from off his sabre-taloned feet,
Uranian sapphires fast in frozen blood,
With amethysts from Mars. I lean to read,   85
With slant-lipped mages, in an evil star,
The monstrous archives of a war that ran
Through wasted aeons, and the prophecy
Of wars renewed, that shall commemorate
Some enmity of wivern-headed kings,   90
Even to the brink of time. I know the blooms
Of bluish fungus, freaked with mercury,
That bloat within the craters of the moon,
And in one still, selenic hour have shrunk
To pools of slime and fetor; and I know   95
What clammy blossoms, blanched and cavern-grown,
Are proffered in Uranus to their gods
By mole-eyed peoples; and the livid seed
Of some black fruit a king in Saturn ate,
Which, cast upon his tinkling palace-floor,   100
Took root between the burnished flags, and now
Hath mounted, and become a hellish tree,
Whose lithe and hairy branches, lined with mouths,
Net like a hundred ropes his lurching throne,
And strain at starting pillars. I behold   105
The slowly-thronging corals, that usurp
Some harbour of a million-masted sea,
And sun them on the league-long wharves of gold—
Bulks of enormous crimson, kraken-limbed
And kraken-headed, lifting up as crowns   110

And plucked from off his saber-taloned feet
Uranian sapphires fast in frozen blood,
And amethysts from Mars. I lean to read   85
With slant-lipped mages, in an evil star,
The monstrous archives of a war that ran
Through wasted eons, and the prophecy
Of wars renewed, which shall commemorate
Some enmity of wivern-headed kings   90
Even to the brink of time. I know the blooms
Of bluish fungus, freaked with mercury,
That bloat within the craters of the moon,
And in one still, selenic hour have shrunk
To pools of slime and fetor; and I know   95
What clammy blossoms, blanched and cavern-grown,
Are proffered to their gods in Uranus
By mole-eyed peoples; and the livid seed
Of some black fruit a king in Saturn ate,
Which, cast upon his tinkling palace-floor,   100
Took root between the burnished flags, and now
Hath mounted and become a hellish tree,
Whose lithe and hairy branches, lined with mouths,
Net like a hundred ropes his lurching throne,
And strain at starting pillars. I behold   105
The slowly-thronging corals that usurp
Some harbor of a million-masted sea,
And sun them on the league-long wharves of gold—
Bulks of enormous crimson, kraken-limbed
And kraken-headed, lifting up as crowns   110

The octiremes of perished emperors,
And galleys fraught with royal gems, that sailed
From a sea-deserted haven.

                Swifter grow
The visions: Now a mighty city looms,
Hewn from a hill of purest cinnabar,   *115*
To domes and turrets like a sunrise thronged
With tier on tier of captive moons, half-drowned
In shifting erubescence. But whose hands
Were sculptors of its doors, and columns wrought
To semblance of prodigious blooms of old,   *120*
No eremite hath lingered there to say,
And no man comes to learn: For long ago
A prophet came, warning its timid king
Against the plague of lichens that had crept
Across subverted empires, and the sand   *125*
Of wastes that Cyclopean mountains ward;
Which, slow and ineluctable, would come,
To take his fiery bastions and his fanes,
And quench his domes with greenish tetter. Now
I see a host of naked giants, armed   *130*
With horns of behemoth and unicorn,
Who wander, blinded by the clinging spells
Of hostile wizardry, and stagger on
To forests where the very leaves have eyes,
And ebonies, like wrathful dragons roar   *135*
To teaks a-chuckle in the loathly gloom;

The octiremes of perished emperors,
And galleys fraught with royal gems, that sailed
From a sea-fled haven.

                             Swifter and stranger grow
The visions: now a mighty city looms,
Hewn from a hill of purest cinnabar   115
To domes and turrets like a sunrise thronged
With tier on tier of captive moons, half-drowned
In shifting erubescence. But whose hands
Were sculptors of its doors, and columns wrought
To semblance of prodigious blooms of old,   120
No eremite hath lingered there to say,
And no man comes to learn: for long ago
A prophet came, warning its timid king
Against the plague of lichens that had crept
Across subverted empires, and the sand   125
Of wastes that cyclopean mountains ward;
Which, slow and ineluctable, would come
To take his fiery bastions and his fanes,
And quench his domes with greenish tetter. Now
I see a host of naked giants, armed   130
With horns of behemoth and unicorn,
Who wander, blinded by the clinging spells
Of hostile wizardry, and stagger on
To forests where the very leaves have eyes,
And ebonies like wrathful dragons roar   135
To teaks a-chuckle in the loathly gloom;

Where coiled lianas lean, with serried fangs,
From writhing palms with swollen boles that moan;
Where leeches of a scarlet moss have sucked
The eyes of some dead monster, and have crawled   *140*
To bask upon his azure-spotted spine;
Where hydra-throated blossoms hiss and sing,
Or yawn with mouths that drip a sluggish dew,
Whose touch is death and slow corrosion. Then,
I watch a war of pigmies, met by night   *145*
With pitter of their drums of parrot's hide,
On plains with no horizon, where a god
Might lose his way for centuries; and there,
In wreathèd light, and fulgors all convolved,
A rout of green, enormous moons ascend,   *150*
With rays that like a shivering venom run
On inch-long swords of lizard-fang.

                    Surveyed
From this my throne, as from a central sun,
The pageantries of worlds and cycles pass;
Forgotten splendours, dream by dream unfold,   *155*
Like tapestry, and vanish; violet suns,
Or suns of changeful iridescence, bring
Their rays about me, like the coloured lights
Imploring priests might lift to glorify
The face of some averted god; the songs   *160*
Of mystic poets in a purple world,
Ascend to me in music that is made

Where coiled lianas lean, with serried fangs,
From writhing palms with swollen boles that moan;
Where leeches of a scarlet moss have sucked
The eyes of some dead monster, and have crawled   *140*
To bask upon his azure-spotted spine;
Where hydra-throated blossoms hiss and sing,
Or yawn with mouths that drip a sluggish dew
Whose touch is death and slow corrosion. Then
I watch a war of pygmies, met by night,   *145*
With pitter of their drums of parrot's hide,
On plains with no horizon, where a god
Might lose his way for centuries; and there,
In wreathèd light and fulgors all convolved,
A rout of green, enormous moons ascend,   *150*
With rays that like a shivering venom run
On inch-long swords of lizard-fang.

                Surveyed
From this my throne, as from a central sun,
The pageantries of worlds and cycles pass;
Forgotten splendors, dream by dream, unfold   *155*
Like tapestry, and vanish; violet suns,
Or suns of changeful iridescence, bring
Their rays about me like the colored lights
Imploring priests might lift to glorify
The face of some averted god; the songs   *160*
Of mystic poets in a purple world
Ascend to me in music that is made

From unconceivèd perfumes, and the pulse
Of love ineffable; the lute-players
Whose lutes are strung with gold of the utmost moon,   *165*
Call forth delicious languors, never known
Save to their golden kings; the sorcerers
Of hooded stars inscrutable to God,
Surrender me their demon-wrested scrolls,
Inscribed with lore of monstrous alchemies,   *170*
And awful transformations. *** If I will,
I am at once the vision and the seer,
And mingle with my ever-streaming pomps,
And still abide their suzerain: I am
The neophyte who serves a nameless god   *175*
Within whose fane the fanes of Hecatompylos
Were arks the Titan worshippers might bear,
Or flags to pave the threshold; or I am
The god himself, who calls the fleeing clouds
Into the nave where suns might congregate,   *180*
And veils the darkling mountain of his face
With fold on solemn fold; for whom the priests
Amass their monthly hecatomb of gems—
Opals that are a camel-cumbering load,
And monstrous alabraundines, won from war   *185*
With realms of hostile serpents; which arise,
Combustible, in vapours many-hued,
And myrrh-excelling perfumes. It is I,
The king, who holds with scepter-dropping hand
The helm of some great barge of chrysolite,   *190*

From unconceivèd perfumes and the pulse
Of love ineffable; the lute-players
Whose lutes are strung with gold of the utmost moon,   *165*
Call forth delicious languors, never known
Save to their golden kings; the sorcerers
Of hooded stars inscrutable to God,
Surrender me their demon-wrested scrolls,
Inscribed with lore of monstrous alchemies   *170*
And awful transformations.

               If I will,
I am at once the vision and the seer,
And mingle with my ever-streaming pomps,
And still abide their suzerain: I am
The neophyte who serves a nameless god,   *175*
Within whose fane the fanes of Hecatompylos
Were arks the Titan worshippers might bear,
Or flags to pave the threshold; or I am
The god himself, who calls the fleeing clouds
Into the nave where suns might congregate   *180*
And veils the darkling mountain of his face
With fold on solemn fold; for whom the priests
Amass their monthly hecatomb of gems—
Opals that are a camel-cumbering load,
And monstrous alabraundines, won from war   *185*
With realms of hostile serpents; which arise,
Combustible, in vapors many-hued
And myrrh-excelling perfumes. It is I,

Sailing upon an amethystine sea
To isles of timeless summer: For the snows
Of hyperborean winter, and their winds,
Sleep in his jewel-builded capital,
Nor any charm of flame-wrought wizardry,   195
Nor conjured suns may rout them; so he flees,
With captive kings to urge his serried oars,
Hopeful of dales where amaranthine dawn
Hath never left the faintly sighing lote
And fields of lisping moly. Or I fare,   200
Impanoplied with azure diamond,
As hero of a quest Achernar lights,
To deserts filled with ever-wandering flames,
That feed upon the sullen marl, and soar
To wrap the slopes of mountains, and to leap,   205
With tongues intolerably lengthening,
That lick the blenchèd heavens. But there lives
(Secure as in a garden walled from wind)
A lonely flower by a placid well,
Midmost the flaring tumult of the flames,   210
That roar as roars the storm-possessèd sea,
Impacable forever: And within
That simple grail the blossom lifts, there lies
One drop of an incomparable dew,
Which heals the parchèd weariness of kings,   215
And cures the wound of wisdom. I am page
To an emperor who reigns ten thousand years,
And through his labyrinthine palace-rooms,

The king, who holds with scepter-dropping hand
The helm of some great barge of orichalchum,   *190*
Sailing upon an amethystine sea
To isles of timeless summer: for the snows
Of hyperborean winter, and their winds,
Sleep in his jewel-builded capital,
Nor any charm of flame-wrought wizardry,   *195*
Nor conjured suns may rout them; so he flees,
With captive kings to urge his serried oars,
Hopeful of dales where amaranthine dawn
Hath never left the faintly sighing lote
And lisping moly. Firm of heart, I fare   *200*
Impanoplied with azure diamond,
As hero of a quest Achernar lights,
To deserts filled with ever-wandering flames
That feed upon the sullen marl, and soar
To wrap the slopes of mountains, and to leap   *205*
With tongues intolerably lengthening
That lick the blenchèd heavens. But there lives
(Secure as in a garden walled from wind)
A lonely flower by a placid well,
Midmost the flaring tumult of the flames,   *210*
That roar as roars a storm-possessèd sea,
Implacable for ever; and within
That simple grail the blossom lifts, there lies
One drop of an incomparable dew
Which heals the parchèd weariness of kings,   *215*
And cures the wound of wisdom. I am page

Through courts and colonnades and balconies
Wherein immensity itself is mazed,   *220*
I seek the golden gorget he hath lost,
On which the names of his conniving stars
Are writ in little sapphires; and I roam
For centuries, and hear the brazen clocks
Innumerably clang with such a sound   *225*
As brazen hammers make, by devils dinned
On tombs of all the dead; and nevermore
I find the gorget, but at length I find
A sealèd room whose nameless prisoner
Moans with a nameless torture, and would turn   *230*
To hell's red rack as to a lilied couch
From that whereon they stretched him; and I find,
Prostrate upon a lotus-painted floor,
The loveliest of all beloved slaves
My emperor hath, and from her pulseless side   *235*
A serpent rises, whiter than the root
Of some venefic bloom in darkness grown,
And gazes up with green-lit eyes that seem
Like drops of cold, congealing poison.***

                                    Hark!
What word was whispered in a tongue unknown,   *240*
In crypts of some impenetrable world?
Whose is the dark, dethroning secrecy
I cannot share, though I am king of suns
And king therewith of strong eternity,

To an emperor who reigns ten thousand years,
And through his labyrinthine palace-rooms,
Through courts and colonnades and balconies
Wherein immensity itself is mazed,   *220*
I seek the golden gorget he hath lost,
On which, in sapphires fine as orris-seed,
Are writ the names of his conniving stars
And friendly planets. Roaming thus, I hear
Like demon tears incessant, through dark ages,   *225*
The drip of sullen clepsydrae; and once
In every lustrum, hear the brazen clocks
Innumerably clang with such a sound
As brazen hammers make, by devils dinned
On tombs of all the dead; and nevermore   *230*
I find the gorget, but at length I find
A sealèd room whose nameless prisoner
Moans with a nameless torture, and would turn
To hell's red rack as to a lilied couch
From that whereon they stretched him; and I find,   *235*
Prostrate upon a lotus-painted floor,
The loveliest of all belovèd slaves
My emperor hath, and from her pulseless side
A serpent rises, whiter than the root
Of some venefic bloom in darkness grown,   *240*
And gazes up with green-lit eyes that seem
Like drops of cold, congealing poison.

Hark!

Whose gnomons with their swords of shadow guard 245
My gates, and slay the intruder? Silence loads
The wind of ether, and the worlds are still
To hear the word that flees me. All my dreams
Fall like a rack of fuming vapours raised
To semblance by a necromant, and leave 250
Spirit and sense unthinkably alone,
Above a universe of shrouded stars,
And suns that wander, cowled with sullen gloom,
Like witches to a Sabbath. *** Fear is born
In crypts below the nadir, and hath crawled 255
Reaching the floor of space and waits for wings
To lift it upward, like a hellish worm
Fain for the flesh of seraphs. Eyes that gleam,
But are not eyes of suns or galaxies,
Gather and throng to the base of darkness; flame 260
Behind some black, abysmal curtain burns,
Implacable, and fanned to whitest wrath
By raisèd wings that flail the whiffled gloom,
And make a brief and broken wind that moans,
As one who rides a throbbing rack. There is 265
A Thing that crouches, worlds and years remote,
Whose horns a demon sharpens, rasping forth
A note to shatter the donjon-keeps of time,
And crack the sphere of crystal. *** All is dark
For ages, and my tolling heart suspends 270
Its clamour, as within the clutch of death,
Tightening with tense, hermetic rigours. Then,

What word was whispered in a tongue unknown,

In crypts of some impenetrable world?

Whose is the dark, dethroning secrecy   245

I cannot share, though I am king of suns,

And king therewith of strong eternity,

Whose gnomons with their swords of shadow guard

My gates, and slay the intruder? Silence loads

The wind of ether, and the worlds are still   250

To hear the word that flees mine audience.

In simultaneous ruin, all my dreams

Fall like a rack of fuming vapors raised

To semblance by a necromant, and leave

Spirit and sense unthinkably alone   255

Above a universe of shrouded stars

And suns that wander, cowled with sullen gloom,

Like witches to a Sabbath. . . . Fear is born

In crypts below the nadir, and hath crawled

Reaching the floor of space, and waits for wings   260

To lift it upward like a hellish worm

Fain for the flesh of cherubim. Red orbs

And eyes that gleam remotely as the stars,

But are not eyes of suns or galaxies,

Gather and throng to the base of darkness; a flame   265

Behind some black, abysmal curtain burns,

Implacable, and fanned to whitest wrath

By raisèd wings that flail the whiffled gloom,

And make a brief and broken wind that moans

As one who rides a throbbing rack. There is   270

In one enormous, million-flashing flame,
The stars unveil, the suns remove their cowls,
And beam to their responding planets; time   275
Is mine once more, and armies of its dreams
Rally to that insuperable throne,
Firmed on the central zenith.

                  Now I seek
The meads of shining moly I had found
In some remoter vision, by a stream   280
No cloud hath ever tarnished; where the sun,
A gold Narcissus, loiters evermore
Above his golden image: But I find
A corpse the ebbing water will not keep,
With eyes like sapphires that have lain in hell,   285
And felt the hissing embers; and the flow'rs
About me turn to hooded serpents, swayed
By flutes of devils in a hellish dance
Meet for the nod of Satan, when he reigns
Above the raging Sabbath, and is wooed   290
By sarabands of witches. But I turn
To mountains guarding with their horns of snow
The source of that befoulèd rill, and seek
A pinnacle where none but eagles climb,
And they with failing pennons. But in vain   295
I flee, for on that pylon of the sky,
Some curse hath turned the unprinted snow to flame—
Red fires that curl and cluster to my tread,

A Thing that crouches, worlds and years remote,
Whose horns a demon sharpens, rasping forth
A note to shatter the donjon-keeps of time,
Or crack the sphere of crystal. All is dark
For ages, and my tolling heart suspends   275
Its clamor as within the clutch of death
Tightening with tense, hermetic rigors. Then,
In one enormous, million-flashing flame,
The stars unveil, the suns remove their cowls,
And beam to their responding planets; time   280
Is mine once more, and armies of its dreams
Rally to that insuperable throne
Firmed on the zenith.

                         Once again I seek
The meads of shining moly I had found
In some anterior vision, by a stream   285
No cloud hath ever tarnished; where the sun,
A gold Narcissus, loiters evermore
Above his golden image. But I find
A corpse the ebbing water will not keep,
With eyes like sapphires that have lain in hell   290
And felt the hissing coals; and all the flowers
About me turn to hooded serpents, swayed
By flutes of devils in lascivious dance
Meet for the nod of Satan, when he reigns
Above the raging Sabbath, and is wooed   295
By sarabands of witches. But I turn

Trying the summit's narrow cirque. And now,
I see a silver python far beneath— 300
Vast as a river that a fiend hath witched,
And forced to flow remèant in its course
To fountains whence it issued. Rapidly
It winds from slope to crumbling slope, and fills
Ravines and chasmal gorges, till the crags 305
Totter with coil on coil incumbent. Soon
It hath entwined the pinnacle I keep,
And gapes with a fanged, unfathomable maw,
Wherein great Typhon, and Enceladus,
Were orts of daily glut. But I am gone, 310
For at my call a hippogriff hath come,
And firm between his thunder-beating wings,
I mount the sheer cerulean walls of noon,
And see the earth, a spurnèd pebble, fall
Lost in the fields of nether stars—and seek 315
A planet where the outwearied wings of time
Might pause and furl for respite, or the plumes
Of death be stayed, and loiter in reprieve
Above some deathless lily: For therein,
Beauty hath found an avatar of flow'rs— 320
Blossoms that clothe it as a coloured flame,
From peak to peak, from pole to sullen pole,
And turn the skies to perfume. There I find
A lonely castle, calm and unbeset,
Save by the purple spears of amaranth, 325
And tender-sworded iris. Walls upbuilt

To mountains guarding with their horns of snow
The source of that befoulèd rill, and seek
A pinnacle where none but eagles climb,
And they with failing pennons. But in vain   300
I flee, for on that pylon of the sky
Some curse hath turned the unprinted snow to flame—
Red fires that curl and cluster to my tread,
Trying the summit's narrow cirque. And now
I see a silver python far beneath—   305
Vast as a river that a fiend hath witched
And forced to flow reverted in its course
To fountains whence it issued. Rapidly
It winds from slope to crumbling slope, and fills
Ravines and chasmal gorges, till the crags   310
Totter with coil on coil incumbent. Soon
It hath entwined the pinnacle I keep,
And gapes with a fanged, unfathomable maw
Wherein great Typhon and Enceladus
Were orts of daily glut. But I am gone,   315
For at my call a hippogriff hath come,
And firm between his thunder-beating wings
I mount the sheer cerulean walls of noon
And see the earth, a spurnèd pebble, fall—
Lost in the fields of nether stars—and seek   320
A planet where the outwearied wings of time
Might pause and furl for respite, or the plumes
Of death be stayed, and loiter in reprieve
Above some deathless lily: for therein

Of flushèd marble, wonderful with rose,
And domes like golden bubbles, and minarets
That take the clouds as coronal—these are mine,
For voiceless looms the peaceful barbican,   330
And the heavy-teethed portcullis hangs aloft
As if to smile a welcome. So I leave
My hippogriff to crop the magic meads,
And pass into a court the lilies hold,
And tread them to a fragrance that pursues   335
To win the portico, whose columns, carved
Of lazuli and amber, mock the palms
Of bright, Aidennic forests—capitalled
With fronds of stone fretted to airy lace,
Enfolding drupes that seem as tawny clusters   340
Of breasts of unknown houris; and convolved
With vines of shut and shadowy-leavèd flow'rs,
Like the dropt lids of women that endure
Some loin-dissolving rapture. Through a door
Enlaid with lilies twined luxuriously,   345
I enter, dazed and blinded with the sun,
And hear, in gloom that changing colours cloud,
A chuckle sharp as crepitating ice,
Upheaved and cloven by shoulders of the damned
Who strive in Antenora. When my eyes   350
Undazzle, and the cloud of colour fades,
I find me in a monster-guarded room,
Where marble apes with wings of griffins crowd
On walls an evil sculptor wrought, and beasts

Beauty hath found an avatar of flowers—   *325*
Blossoms that clothe it as a colored flame
From peak to peak, from pole to sullen pole,
And turn the skies to perfume. There I find
A lonely castle, calm, and unbeset
Save by the purple spears of amaranth,   *330*
And leafing iris tender-sworded. Walls
Of flushèd marble, wonderful with rose,
And domes like golden bubbles, and minarets
That take the clouds as coronal—these are mine,
For voiceless looms the peaceful barbican,   *335*
And the heavy-teethed portcullis hangs aloft
To grin a welcome. So I leave awhile
My hippogriff to crop the magic meads,
And pass into a court the lilies hold,
And tread them to a fragrance that pursues   *340*
To win the portico, whose columns, carved
Of lazuli and amber, mock the palms
Of bright Aidennic forests—capitalled
With fronds of stone fretted to airy lace,
Enfolding drupes that seem as tawny clusters   *345*
Of breasts of unknown houris; and convolved
With vines of shut and shadowy-leavèd flowers
Like the dropt lids of women that endure
Some loin-dissolving ecstasy. Through doors
Enlaid with lilies twined luxuriously,   *350*
I enter, dazed and blinded with the sun,
And hear, in gloom that changing colors cloud,

Wherein the sloth and vampire-bat unite,   355
Pendulous by their toes of tarnished bronze,
Usurp the shadowy interval of lamps
That hang from ebon arches. Like a ripple,
Borne by the wind from pool to sluggish pool
In fields where wide Cocytus flows his bound,   360
A crackling smile around that circle runs,
And all the stone-wrought gibbons stare at me
With eyes that turn to glowing coals. A fear
That found no name in Babel, flings me on,
Breathless and faint with horror, to a hall   365
Within whose weary, self-reverting round,
The languid curtains, heavier than palls,
Unnumerably depict a weary king,
Who fain would cool his jewel-crusted hands
In lakes of emerald evening, or the fields   370
Of dreamless poppies pure with rain. I flee
Onward, and all the shadowy curtains shake
With tremors of a silken-sighing mirth,
And whispers of the innumerable king,
Breathing a tale of ancient pestilence,   375
Whose very words are vile contagion. Then
I reach a room where caryatides,
Carved in the form of tall, voluptuous Titan women,
Surround a throne of flowering ebony
Where creeps a vine of crystal. On the throne,   380
There lolls a wan, enormous Worm, whose bulk,
Tumid with all the rottenness of kings,

A chuckle sharp as crepitating ice
Upheaved and cloven by shoulders of the damned
Who strive in Antenora. When my eyes   355
Undazzle, and the cloud of color fades,
I find me in a monster-guarded room,
Where marble apes with wings of griffins crowd
On walls an evil sculptor wrought; and beasts
Wherein the sloth and vampire-bat unite,   360
Pendulous by their toes of tarnished bronze,
Usurp the shadowy interval of lamps
That hang from ebon arches. Like a ripple
Borne by the wind from pool to sluggish pool
In fields where wide Cocytus flows his bound,   365
A crackling smile around that circle runs,
And all the stone-wrought gibbons stare at me
With eyes that turn to glowing coals. A fear
That found no name in Babel, flings me on,
Breathless and faint with horror, to a hall   370
Within whose weary, self-reverting round,
The languid curtains, heavier than palls,
Unnumerably depict a weary king
Who fain would cool his jewel-crusted hands
In lakes of emerald evening, or the fields   375
Of dreamless poppies pure with rain. I flee
Onward, and all the shadowy curtains shake
With tremors of a silken-sighing mirth,
And whispers of the innumerable king,
Breathing a tale of ancient pestilence   380

O'erflows its arms with fold on creasèd fold
Of fat obscenely bloating. Open-mouthed
He leans, and from his throat a score of tongues,   385
Depending like to wreaths of torpid vipers,
Drivel with phosphorescent slime, that runs
Down all his length of soft and monstrous folds,
And creeping among the flow'rs of ebony,
Lends them the life of tiny serpents. Now,   390
Ere the Horror ope those red and lashless slits
Of eyes that draw the gnat and midge, I turn,
And follow down a dusty hall, whose gloom,
Lined by the statues with their mighty limbs,
Ends in a golden-roofèd balcony   395
Sphering the flowered horizon.

                              Ere my heart
Hath hushed the panic tumult of its pulses,
I listen, from beyond the horizon's rim,
A mutter faint as when the far simoon,
Mounting from unknown deserts, opens forth,   400
Wide as the waste, those wings of torrid night
That fling the doom of cities from their folds,
And musters in its van a thousand winds,
That with disrooted palms for besoms, rise
And sweep the sands to fury. As the storm,   405
Approaching, mounts and loudens to the ears
Of them that toil in fields of sesame,
So grows the mutter, and a shadow creeps

Whose very words are vile contagion. Then
I reach a room where caryatides,
Carved in the form of voluptuous Titan women,
Surround a throne of flowering ebony
Where creeps a vine of crystal. On the throne   385
There lolls a wan, enormous Worm, whose bulk,
Tumid with all the rottenness of kings,
Overflows its arms with fold on creasèd fold
Obscenely bloating. Open-mouthed he leans,
And from his fulvous throat a score of tongues,   390
Depending like to wreaths of torpid vipers,
Drivel with phosphorescent slime, that runs
Down all his length of soft and monstrous folds,
And creeping among the flowers of ebony,
Lends them the life of tiny serpents. Now,   395
Ere the Horror ope those red and lashless slits
Of eyes that draw the gnat and midge, I turn
And follow down a dusty hall, whose gloom,
Lined by the statues with their mighty limbs,
Ends in a golden-roofèd balcony   400
Sphering the flowered horizon.

                                     Ere my heart
Hath hushed the panic tumult of its pulses,
I listen, from beyond the horizon's rim,
A mutter faint as when the far simoon,
Mounting from unknown deserts, opens forth,   405
Wide as the waste, those wings of torrid night

Above the gold horizon, like a dawn
Of darkness climbing sunward. Now they come,   410
A Sabbath of abominable shapes,
Led by the fiends and lamiae of worlds
That owned my sway aforetime! Cockatrice,
Python, tragelaphus, leviathan,
Chimera, martichoras, behemoth,   415
Geryon and sphinx, and hydra, on my ken
Arise as might some Afrite-builded city,
Consummate in the lifting of a lash,
With thundrous domes and sounding obelisks,
And towers of night and fire alternate! Wings   420
Of white-hot stone along the hissing wind,
Bear up the huge and furnace-hearted beasts
Of hells beyond Rutilicus; and things
Whose lightless length would mete the gyre of moons—
Born from the caverns of a dying sun,   425
Uncoil to the very zenith, half disclosed
From gulfs below the horizon; octopi
Like blazing moons with countless arms of fire,
Climb from the seas of ever-surging flame
That roll and roar through planets unconsumed,   430
Beating on coasts of unknown metals; beasts
That range the mighty worlds of Alioth, rise,
Aforesting the heavens with multitudinous horns,
Within whose maze the winds are lost; and borne
On cliff-like brows of plunging scolopendras,   435
The shell-wrought tow'rs of ocean-witches loom,

That shake the doom of cities from their folds,
And musters in its van a thousand winds
That, with disrooted palms for besoms, rise,
And sweep the sands to fury. As the storm,   410
Approaching, mounts and loudens to the ears
Of them that toil in fields of sesame,
So grows the mutter, and a shadow creeps
Above the gold horizon like a dawn
Of darkness climbing zenith-ward. They come,   415
The Sabaoth of retribution, drawn
From all dread spheres that knew my trespassing,
And led by vengeful fiends and dire alastors
That owned my sway aforetime! Cockatrice,
Python, tragelaphus, leviathan,   420
Chimera, martichoras, behemoth,
Geryon, and sphinx, and hydra, on my ken
Arise as might some Afrit-builded city
Consummate in the lifting of a lash
With thunderous domes and sounding obelisks   425
And towers of night and fire alternate! Wings
Of white-hot stone along the hissing wind
Bear up the huge and furnace-hearted beasts
Of hells beyond Rutilicus; and things
Whose lightless length would mete the gyre of moons—   430
Born from the caverns of a dying sun—
Uncoil to the very zenith, half-disclosed
From gulfs below the horizon; octopi
Like blazing moons with countless arms of fire,

And griffin-mounted gods, and demons throned
On sable dragons, and the cockodrills
That bear the spleenful pygmies on their backs;
And blue-faced wizards from the worlds of Saiph,   440
On whom Titanic scorpions fawn; and armies
That move with fronts reverted from the foe,
And strike athwart their shoulders at the shapes
Their shields reflect in crystal; and eidola
Fashioned within unfathomable caves   445
By hands of eyeless peoples; and the blind
And worm-shaped monsters of a sunless world,
With krakens from the ultimate abyss,
And Demogorgons of the outer dark,
Arising, shout with multitudinous thunders,   450
And threatening me with dooms ineffable
In words whereat the heavens leap to flame,
Advance on the magic palace! Thrown before,
For league on league, their blasting shadows blight
And eat like fire the amaranthine meads,   455
Leaving an ashen desert! In the palace,
I hear the apes of marble shriek and howl,
And all the women-shapen columns moan,
Babbling with unknown terror. In my fear,
A monstrous dread unnamed in any hell,   460
I rise, and flee with the fleeing wind for wings,
And in a trice the magic palace reels,
And spiring to a single tow'r of flame,
Goes out, and leaves nor shard nor ember! Flown

Climb from the seas of ever-surging flame   435
That roll and roar through planets unconsumed,
Beating on coasts of unknown metals; beasts
That range the mighty worlds of Alioth rise,
Afforesting the heavens with multitudinous horns
Amid whose maze the winds are lost; and borne   440
On cliff-like brows of plunging scolopendras,
The shell-wrought towers of ocean-witches loom;
And griffin-mounted gods, and demons throned
On sable dragons, and the cockodrills
That bear the spleenful pygmies on their backs;   445
And blue-faced wizards from the worlds of Saiph,
On whom Titanic scorpions fawn; and armies
That move with fronts reverted from the foe,
And strike athwart their shoulders at the shapes
Their shields reflect in crystal; and eidola   450
Fashioned within unfathomable caves
By hands of eyeless peoples; and the blind
Worm-shapen monsters of a sunless world,
With krakens from the ultimate abyss,
And Demogorgons of the outer dark,   455
Arising, shout with dire multisonous clamors,
And threatening me with dooms ineffable
In words whereat the heavens leap to flame,
Advance upon the enchanted palace. Falling
For league on league before, their shadows blight   460
And eat like fire the amaranthine meads,
Leaving an ashen desert. In the palace

Beyond the world, upon that fleeing wind,   465
I reach the gulf's irrespirable verge,
Where fails the strongest storm for breath and fall,
Supportless, through the nadir-plungèd gloom,
Beyond the scope and vision of the sun,
To other skies and systems. In a world   470
Deep-wooded with the multi-coloured fungi,
That soar to semblance of fantastic palms,
I fall as falls the meteor-stone, and break
A score of trunks to powder. All unhurt,
I rise, and through the illimitable woods,   475
Among the trees of flimsy opal, roam,
And see their tops that clamber, hour by hour,
To touch the suns of iris. Things unseen,
Whose charnel breath informs the tideless air
With spreading pools of fetor, follow me   480
Elusive past the ever-changing palms;
And pittering moths, with wide and ashen wings,
Flit on before, and insects ember-hued,
Descending, hurtle through the gorgeous gloom,
And quench themselves in crumbling thickets. Heard   485
Far-off, the gong-like roar of beasts unknown
Resounds at measured intervals of time,
Shaking the riper trees to dust, that falls
In clouds of acrid perfume, stifling me
Beneath a pall of iris.

Now the palms   490

I hear the apes of marble shriek and howl,
And all the women-shapen columns moan,
Babbling with terror. In my tenfold fear,   465
A monstrous dread unnamed in any hell,
I rise, and flee with the fleeing wind for wings,
And in a trice the wizard palace reels,
And spiring to a single tower of flame,
Goes out, and leaves nor shard nor ember! Flown   470
Beyond the world upon that fleeing wind
I reach the gulf's irrespirable verge,
Where fails the strongest storm for breath, and fall,
Supportless, through the nadir-plungèd gloom,
Beyond the scope and vision of the sun,   475
To other skies and systems.

                                  In a world
Deep-wooded with the multi-colored fungi
That soar to semblance of fantastic palms,
I fall as falls the meteor-stone, and break
A score of trunks to atom-powder. Unharmed   480
I rise, and through the illimitable woods,
Among the trees of flimsy opal, roam,
And see their tops that clamber hour by hour
To touch the suns of iris. Things unseen,
Whose charnel breath informs the tideless air   485
With spreading pools of fetor, follow me,
Elusive past the ever-changing palms;
And pittering moths with wide and ashen wings

Grow far apart and lessen momently
To shrubs a dwarf might topple. Over them
I see an empty desert, all ablaze
With amethysts and rubies, and the dust
Of garnets or carnelians. On I roam,   495
Treading the gorgeous grit, that dazzles me
With leaping waves of endless rutilance,
Whereby the air is turned to a crimson gloom,
Through which I wander, blind as any Kobold;
Till underfoot the grinding sands give place   500
To stone or metal, with a massive ring
More welcome to mine ears than golden bells,
Or tinkle of silver fountains. When the gloom
Of crimson lifts, I stand upon the edge
Of a broad black plain of adamant, that reaches,   505
Level as windless water, to the verge
Of all the world; and through the sable plain,
A hundred streams of shattered marble run,
And streams of broken steel, and streams of bronze,
Like to the ruin of all the wars of time,   510
To plunge, with clangour of timeless cataracts
Adown the gulfs eternal.

So I follow,
Between a river of steel and a river of bronze,
With ripples loud and tuneless as the clash
Of a million lutes; and come to the precipice   515
From which they fall, and make the mighty sound

Flit on before, and insects ember-hued,
Descending, hurtle through the gorgeous gloom   490
And quench themselves in crumbling thickets. Heard
Far off, the gong-like roar of beasts unknown
Resounds at measured intervals of time,
Shaking the riper trees to dust, that falls
In clouds of acrid perfume, stifling me   495
Beneath an irised pall.

                            Now the palmettoes
Grow far apart, and lessen momently
To shrubs a dwarf might topple. Over them
I see an empty desert, all ablaze
With amethysts and rubies, and the dust   500
Of garnets or carnelians. On I roam,
Treading the gorgeous grit, that dazzles me
With leaping waves of endless rutilance,
Whereby the air is turned to a crimson gloom
Through which I wander blind as any Kobold;   505
Till underfoot the grinding sands give place
To stone or metal, with a massive ring
More welcome to mine ears than golden bells
Or tinkle of silver fountains. When the gloom
Of crimson lifts, I stand upon the edge   510
Of a broad black plain of adamant that reaches,
Level as windless water, to the verge
Of all the world; and through the sable plain
A hundred streams of shattered marble run,

Of a million swords that meet a million shields,
Or din of spears and armour in the wars
Of all the worlds and aeons: Far beneath,
They fall, through gulfs and cycles of the void,   520
And vanish like a stream of broken stars,
Into the nether darkness; nor the gods
Of any sun, nor demons of the gulf,
Will dare to know what everlasting sea
Is fed thereby, and mounts forevermore   525
With mighty tides unebbing.

             Lo, what cloud,
Or night of sudden and supreme eclipse,
Is on the suns of opal? At my side,
The rivers run with a wan and ghostly gleam,
Through darkness falling as the night that falls   530
From mighty spheres extinguished! Turning now,
I see, betwixt the desert and the suns,
The poisèd wings of all the dragon-rout,
Far-flown in black occlusion thousand-fold
Through stars, and deeps, and devastated worlds,   535
Upon my trail of terror! Griffins, rocs,
And sluggish, dark chimeras, heavy-winged
After the ravin of dispeopled lands,
With harpies, and the vulture-birds of hell—
Hot from abominable feasts and fain   540
To cool their beaks and talons in my blood—
All, all have gathered, and the wingless rear,

And streams of broken steel, and streams of bronze,   *515*
Like to the ruin of all the wars of time,
To plunge with clangor of timeless cataracts
Adown the gulfs eternal.

So I follow
Between a river of steel and a river of bronze,
With ripples loud and tuneless as the clash   *520*
Of a million lutes; and come to the precipice
From which they fall, and make the mighty sound
Of a million swords that meet a million shields,
Or din of spears and armor in the wars
Of half the worlds and eons. Far beneath   *525*
They fall, through gulfs and cycles of the void,
And vanish like a stream of broken stars
Into the nether darkness; nor the gods
Of any sun, nor demons of the gulf,
Will dare to know what everlasting sea   *530*
Is fed thereby, and mounts forevermore
In one unebbing tide.

What nimbus-cloud
Or night of sudden and supreme eclipse,
Is on the suns of opal? At my side
The rivers run with a wan and ghostly gleam   *535*
Through darkness falling as the night that falls
From spheres extinguished. Turning, I behold
Betwixt the sable desert and the suns,

With rank on rank of foul, colossal Worms,
Like pillars of embattled night and flame,
Looms on the wide horizon! From the van   545
I hear the shriek of wyvers, loud and shrill
As tempests in a broken fane, and roar
Of sphinxes, like the unrelenting toll
Of bells from tow'rs infernal. Cloud on cloud,
They arch the zenith, and a dreadful wind   550
Falls from them like the wind before the storm.
And in the wind my cloven garment streams,
And flutters in the face of all the void,
Even as flows a flaffing spirit, lost
On the Pit's undying tempest! Louder grows   555
The thunder of the streams of stone and bronze—
Redoubled with the roar of torrent wings,
Inseparably mingled. Scarce I keep
My footing, in the gulfward winds of fear,
And mighty thunders, beating to the void   560
In sea-like waves incessant; and would flee
With them, and prove the nadir-founded night
Where fall the streams of ruin; but when I reach
The verge, and seek through sun-defeating gloom,
To measure with my gaze the dread descent,   565
I see a tiny star within the depths—
A light that stays me, while the wings of doom
Convene their thickening thousands: For the star
Increases, taking to its hueless orb,
With all the speed of horror-changèd dreams,   570

The poisèd wings of all the dragon-rout,
Far-flown in black occlusion thousand-fold   540
Through stars, and deeps, and devastated worlds,
Upon my trail of terror! Griffins, rocs,
And sluggish, dark chimeras, heavy-winged
After the ravin of dispeopled lands,
And harpies, and the vulture-birds of hell,   545
Hot from abominable feasts, and fain
To cool their beaks and talons in my blood—
All, all have gathered, and the wingless rear,
With rank on rank of foul, colossal Worms,
Makes horrent now the horizon. From the van   550
I hear the shriek of wyvers, loud and shrill
As tempests in a broken fane, and roar
Of sphinxes, like relentless toll of bells
From towers infernal. Cloud on hellish cloud
They arch the zenith, and a dreadful wind   555
Falls from them like the wind before the storm,
And in the wind my riven garment streams
And flutters in the face of all the void,
Even as flows a flaffing spirit, lost
On the pit's undying tempest. Louder grows   560
The thunder of the streams of stone and bronze—
Redoubled with the roar of torrent wings
Inseparably mingled. Scarce I keep
My footing in the gulfward winds of fear,
And mighty thunders beating to the void   565
In sea-like waves incessant; and would flee

The light as of a million million moons;
And floating up through gulfs and glooms eclipsed,
It grows and grows, a huge white eyeless Face,
That fills the void and fills the universe,
And bloats against the limits of the world   575
With lips of flame that open. ****

With them, and prove the nadir-founded night
Where fall the streams of ruin. But when I reach
The verge, and seek through sun-defeating gloom
To measure with my gaze the dread descent,   570
I see a tiny star within the depths—
A light that stays me while the wings of doom
Convene their thickening thousands: for the star
Increases, taking to its hueless orb,
With all the speed of horror-changèd dreams,   575
The light as of a million million moons;
And floating up through gulfs and glooms eclipsed
It grows and grows, a huge white eyeless Face
That fills the void and fills the universe,
And bloats against the limits of the world   580
With lips of flame that open. . . .

COMMENTARY

Glossary

Most of the following information has been taken from *Webster's New Collegiate Dictionary* (ninth edition), *Webster's Unabridged Dictionary* (i.e., *Webster's New International Dictionary*, current edition), the *Oxford English Dictionary* (current edition), and various encyclopaedias, including those dealing with astronomy, geology, and mythology (current as of 1990). Line numbers are keyed to the *Ebony and Crystal* text, except as noted.

Title: 2nd or alternative title: apocalypse: revelation] The uncovering, unfolding, unsealing, revealing: as in the last book of the New Testament, the *Apocalypse*, otherwise known as *The Revelation of Saint John the Divine*; any prophetic revelation.

5 zenith] That point of the heavens, or the celestial vertically above one; the upper pole of the horizon, and opposite to the nadir; the highest point or place. (Compare with *nadir* in line 255.)

7 rampant] Rearing up on the hind legs: a term and position especially used in heraldry.

glut] Prey or food.

11 adamant] An imaginary substance of impenetrable hardness, metal or stone, or a fusion of both; formerly, the diamond.

12 lava-langued] Lava-tongued.

19 fulvous] Dull yellow.

20 runes] As used here, curious characters of a secret mysterious language.

21 sirens] in Greek mythology, enticing but perilous creatures, part woman and part bird, that lure humans to their ruin or death.

25	antic] Originally, antique: grotesquely or ludicrously fantastic in appearance or behavior.
	gnomes] A fabulous race of short underground beings, guardians of mines, quarries, etc.
	abominably] Abominable: hateful, detestable, loathsome, disgusting.
30	glyphs] Pictographs or letters of an alphabet.
31	torrid] Extremely hot.
35	avatars] An avatar is an incarnation, an embodiment, a manifestation: possibly meaning, in this context, the innumerable incarnations undergone by the dreamer or visionary, the hero of the poem.
36	Promethèan] Usually Promèthean. Like Prometheus: hence, life-giving, daring, original, creative; in this context, the armies of entities created by the dreamer, godlike, in the act of dreaming or thinking.
37	levins] Lighting bolts.
40	Armageddon] A great battle to be fought, during "the great day of God" (Rev. 16:14), between the powers of good and evil; hence, any great final battle or struggle between opposing forces.
46	ineffable] Beyond expression or description.
48	Asmodai] Asmodeus: in Jewish demonology, an evil spirit; later, the king of the demons.
	Set] In Egyptian mythology, the god of evil.
49	seventh paradise] Or seventh heaven. In Islam, the last and highest of the abodes of bliss; hence, a state of extreme rapture, of joy supreme.
50	culminant] Culminating.
53	star-unwinnowed] Not winnowed or dispersed with stars.
55	Babel] Sometimes used as synonymous with Babylon and the Hanging Gardens. A structure impossibly huge or lofty; or a city and tower in the land of Shinar, the scene of the confusion of languages, as described in Genesis.

56	their myriad witness] The dreamer perceives all these visions all at once or in a series, one after another.
57	Ombos] Possibly, Kom Ombo: an ancient city on the Nile River in southern or upper Egypt; or Smith may mean some other site in the ancient Mediterranean world, a real place, or a mythical one extrapolated therefrom, otherwise untraceable.
57	Titans] In Greek mythology, the primaeval deities, children of Ouranos and Gaia, displaced by the twelve Olympians.
64	basilisk] A fabulous or imaginary serpent, lizard, or dragon whose breath, or even look, was fatal; see also cockatrice in line 413.
65	upas] In Malay, *pohon upas*, or tree of poison. Either of two trees in Java that yield an intensely poisonous milky substance, i.e., juice.
66	litten] Lit or lighted.
69	torpid] Sluggish, dull, not animated.
73	sphinx] A fabulous monster having wings, a lion's body, and the head and bust of a human female.
75	gall] Bile: the yellow or greenish viscid fluid secreted by the liver; it would make a curious ink with which to write.
	chimeras, chimaeras] Chimera: generally, any imaginary monster; specifically, in Greek mythology, a she-monster belching flames and possessing a lion's head, a goat's body, and a serpent's or a dragon's tail.
76	pentacles] A pentacle is a certain figure used as a magic symbol, such as a five- or six-pointed star, by magicians, wizards, etc.; but pentacles also seem to be used by some writers of imaginative stories or poems to mean a certain kind of heavy tome secured with at least five locks.
	lunar] Pertaining to the moon.
77	roc] In Arabian mythology, a fabulous bird of Arabia so huge that it bears off elephants to feed its young.
79	alabaster mount] A mountain made up entirely of alabaster, sometimes mentioned as a kind of marble (which is a variety of limestone); but alabaster itself is a variety of gypsum, usually a white mineral sometimes used as a decorative stone or sometimes reduced

to a powder and made into various compounds or compositions. A mountain composed entirely of alabaster would indicate such an enormous deposit of gypsum as could exist only in fable or mythology. (Compare to "the hill of purest cinnabar" in line 115.)

90   wivern-headed kings] A wivern, or wyvern, is a fabulous two-legged winged creature, like a cockatrice (in line 413), but having a dragon's head, and a serpent's tail with barbed end.

92   freaked] Streaked.

94   selenic] Lunar.

95   fetor] Stench.

97   Uranus] In Greek mythology, the personification of Heaven; in astronomy, a planet contained in our own solar system, often pronounced "ùranus" or "urànus" (the latter incorrectly). See H. P. Lovecraft's query to Smith regarding pronunciation, *Selected Letters: 1911–1924* (Sauk City, WI: Arkham House, 1965), p. 214. Smith revised the line for the appearance in *Selected Poems*. For obvious reasons, the Late Latin word has been changed back to the original Greek form of Ouranos, i.e., in our own pronunciation.

109   kraken] A fabulous Norwegian sea monster, possibly similar to a giant squid or octopus.

111   octireme] A word coined (evidently by Smith) on the analogy of unireme, bireme, trireme, etc., galleys with one, two, or three banks of oars on either side, respectively; hence, an octireme would possess eight banks of oars on either side.

115   cinnabar] The color vermilion, vermillion. Red mercuric sulfide, the only important ore of mercury, used as a pigment, bright-red in color: "a mighty city . . . / Hewn from a hill of purest cinnabar" thus betokens such an enormous amount of cinnabar as could exist only in fable or mythology. (Compare to the alabaster mountain in line 79.)

118   erubescence] Rubescence: state or condition of growing or becoming or simply being red or, in this context, a state or condition of intensifying the redness already there.

121   eremite] Hermit.

126 Cyclopean] Pertaining to the race of one-eyed giants, or Cyclopes, each having one eye in the middle of the forehead; hence, of a particularly awesome hugeness.

127 ineluctable] Inescapable, unavoidable.

128 fanes] Temples.

129 with greenish tetter] As though the buildings of the mighty city hewn from the hill of purest cinnabar could be attacked by a disease like that which attacks human skin, a disease such as ringworm, eczema, erysipelas, etc.—because of the motley and variegated character of the markings affecting the skin, or (in this instance) evidently the architectural surfaces, the visual effect for a dispassionate onlooker, regardless of the cause, would be extremely colorful and picturesque.

131 behemoth] Pronounced both "behèmoth" and "bèhemoth"— Hebrew (intensive) plural for beast; a real or a fabulous monster, either the hippopotamus or an especially large hippopotamuslike creature.

136 loathly] Loathsome.

142 hydra-throated blossoms] A phrase made on the analogy of hydra-headed monsters. In Greek mythology, a hydra is a monster with nine heads, any of which, when cut off, would be replaced by two others, unless the wound was cauterized. The image intended here could be that of an enormous half-sentient flower sporting a myriad of other flowers; hence, a weird floral monstrosity.

145 pigmies] Pygmies: a fabled race of dwarves as described by the ancient Greek authors.

146 pitter] Similar to patter, as in pitter-patter. A rapid series of light sounds or beats.

149 fulgors] A fulgor is a splendor, or a dazzling brightness.

157 changeful iridescence] State or condition of being rainbow- or multi-colored, i.e., shifting from one color to another.

170 monstrous alchemies] Frightening chemical changes, or alchemies, chemistries, or physical processes that create monstrous beings or conditions.

171   awful transformations] The reference here is possibly to the series of lives or incarnations undergone by the individual soul or spirit. For example, it could be that the entity while yet alive in one shape might be transformed into another and even more loathsome one.

174   suzerain] Sovereign; supreme ruler.

175   neophyte] A new convert to some religion or form of worship.

176   Hecatompylos] A name for Thebes in Egypt meaning hundred gates—a reference to the multiplicity of huge temples there, most being approached through large and impressive pylons or gates; not the Hecatompylos, the ancient Parthian city, lying somewhat near the southern end of the Caspian Sea.

183   hecatomb] In Greek antiquity, literally a sacrifice of one hundred oxen or cattle all at one time; hence, any great sacrifice or offering to a god or gods.

185   alabraundines] Like alabaunderrynes, a mediaeval form or spelling of almandines or almandites. An especially beautiful deep-red or violet-hued variety of garnet, much esteemed as a gem by the Greeks and Romans, and still used in jewelry today. All the various forms or spellings derive from the Latin word alabandina, after Alabanda, the ancient Greek town in Caria, Asia Minor, whence the gems were exported to the ancient Mediterranean world.

190   chrysolite] A mineral, olive-green in color, transparent varieties of which are used as gems: a barge made entirely of chrysolite, if it could float, would constitute a most beautiful vessel, even if rather curious.

191   amethystine] Pertaining to the amethyst. A clear purple or blue-violet variety of crystallized quartz; also a blue-purple sapphire.

193   hyperborean] Pertaining to the far north.

198   amaranthine] An empurpled rose color; also, unfading, undying, eternal. The amaranth itself is both a fabulous or imaginary flower and a real plant whose seeds are used as a grain.

199   lote] Lotus: various flowering water plants not dissimilar in appearance to water lilies, but not necessarily the same as them. The lote tree is the Jujube tree, identified with the tree that bore the mythical lotus-fruit.

200	moly] A fabulous herb of occult power, mentioned by Homer, Milton, and other poets.
201	impanoplied] Covered and protected by some form of magnificent armor; literally, dressed in full armor.
202	Achernar] Word of Arabic origin. The brightest star in the constellation Eridanus.
204	marl] A type of earth made up mostly of clay, and used as a fertilizer; simply, earth. Sullen marl would be a particularly dark type of earth.
207	blenchèd] Blanchèd: grown or made pale or white.
212	implacable] Not to be placated, appeased, or pacified; inexorable.
213	grail] A kind of cup.
221	gorget] A kind of covering, or piece of jewelry, worn on the neck, throat, or breast, similar to a pectoral or breastplate.
222	[EC] the names of his conniving stars] Apparently, if thus recorded in such relatively permanent materials, this phrase would indicate an immutable horoscope and, hence, an unavoidable destiny.
222	[SP] orris-seed] The seed of *Iris florentine*, a European species of iris.
226	[SP] clepsydrae] Water clocks. A clepsydra is a kind of clock that measures time by the fall, or flux, of some quantity of water.
231	rack] A bed or engine of torture upon which the victim was fastened and literally stretched.
237	venefic] Poison-producing, or poisonous.
245	gnomons] Literally, those who know; hence, in this context, especially alert or cognizant guards or guardians, not necessarily the same as gnomes in line 25.
247	the wind of ether] Ether: the non-material substance once thought to fill space. Hence, the wind or winds blowing between the planets, stars, galaxies, etc.—the wind that roams the cosmos.
249	rack] A different rack from the one mentioned in lines 231 and 265. Here, a mass or other arrangement of clouds or vapor; a faint trace; a vestige.

250 necromant] Necromancer: one who divines the future with the aid of the dead, or who brings the dead to life; hence, necromancy is magic or conjuration in general.

254 Sabbath] Always used in this poem with the meaning of a witches' Sabbath. In mediaeval demonology, the usually midnight gathering at which demons, witches, and sorcerers were presumed to celebrate their orgies, usually in the form of an unholy mass, obviously imitating the regular Christian mass, but in a deliberately inverted manner.

255 nadir] That point of the heavens, or the celestial sphere, directly under the place where one stands; the inferior pole or place. (Compare with *zenith* in line 5.)

258 fain] Ready, desirous, eager.

seraphs] In Jewish religious thought, an order of celestial beings, conceived as fiery and purifying ministers of Jehovah. The seraphs, or seraphim, are usually ranked as the highest order of angels, and hence just above the cherubim.

261 abysmal] See *abyss* in line 448.

263 flail] Beat or whip.

whiffled gloom] Darkness in which the air or the wind blows unsteadily or in spasmodic gusts.

268 donjon-keeps] A redundant or intensive form: donjon or keep, the main part of a fortified castle, usually a massive tower, here used as a symbol for something otherwise impregnable or unconquerable.

272 rigours] Rigor: convulsive tremor, contraction, stiffening, shivering, etc., here involving extreme paln or agony, as in a fatal or near-fatal heart attack.

277 insuperable] Than which nothing can be higher.

279 meads] Meadows.

291 sarabands] Originally, a saraband was a rude and lively Spanish dance, performed with castanets; later, a slow and stately court dance derived from the original one, and fashionable during the seventeenth and eighteenth centuries. Any "sarabands of witches"

taking place at a "raging Sabbath" would obviously indicate some aptly rude and lively dancing performed with noticeable speed.

296   pylon] Gate or tower; here, a tower.

299   cirque] Circle.

300   python] A large snake, or in Greek mythology, a monstrous or incredibly large serpent.

306   incumbent] Impending: lying upon something with downward pressure.

309   Typhon] In Greek and Roman mythology, a monster who was originally the son of Typhoeus, but who later became identified with Typhoeus himself. In Greek mythology, Typhoeus was a rather large monster possessing a hundred heads with frightful eyes and voices.

       Enceladus] In Greek mythology, one of the hundred-armed giants who warred against the twelve Olympians, and who was overthrown by Pallas Athena.

310   orts] Bits and pieces of a meal, or as left over from a meal.

       daily glut] Ordinary consumption on a large scale.

311   hippogriff] A fabulous winged animal, half horse and half griffin (see note on line 353).

313   cerulean] Deep blue or azure.

330   barbican] Usually, a tower or towers at a gate or a bridge, often as part of the outer defenses of a city or a castle.

331   portcullis] A stout grating of iron, hung in or over the gateway of a fortress or a castle, to be let down to prevent entrance.

337   lazuli] Lapis lazuli: a stone of a rich azure-blue color.

338   Aidennic] Edenic, or paradisal.

341   drupes] Drupe: a fleshy fruit, such as the plum, peach, date, etc., usually having a single hard stone.

341   houris] Nymphs residing in the Islamic paradise.

348   crepitating] Crackling: cracking or breaking with small, sharp, sudden, repeated noises, often said of pack ice.

350   Antenora] A name given by Dante (in *The Divine Comedy*) to the second zone of Cocytus (ninth circle of the Inferno), to which have been condemned those persons who have betrayed their own country or their own immediate group (family, political party, etc.), and who are fastened onto the ice with their bodies but not with their heads. The name was evidently derived from that of Antenor (in Italian, Antenore), the Trojan hero (who appears in Homer's *Iliad; not* the Athenian sculptor of the same name who lived during the 6th century B.C.E.). (Translated and adapted from the *Lessico Universale Italiano*, Vol. I, p. 176.)

353   griffins] Griffin, gryphon: in Greek mythology, a monster half lion and half eagle.

356   pendulous] Hanging or swinging.

360   Cocytus] In Greek mythology, a river tributory to the Acheron in Hades.

362   gibbons] Small apes with slender bodies and long arms.

377   caryatides] Columns fashioned in the shape of women.

382   tumid] Swollen, enlarged, inflated.

392   midge] Any very small gnat or fly.

399   simoon] A hot, dry, violent wind full of dust that blows on occasion in Arabia, Syria, the Sahara in North Africa, etc.—in short, an arid, very strong desert storm.

401   torrid night] Night characterized by burning or scorching heat.

404   besoms] Brooms made from twigs.

412   lamiae] Lamia: one of a class of man-devouring monsters, possessing the head and breast of a woman together with the body of a serpent; also, a vampire, witch, or sorceress. Generally, any bizarre and life-threatening monster.

413   cockatrice] A fabulous serpent with deadly glance, said to be hatched by a reptile from a cock's egg; also imaged, in heraldry, as a cocklike two-legged winged creature with a dragon's tail. See also *basilisk* in line 64. (The cockatrice is often confused with the basilisk, or basiliskos, diminutive form of basileus, or king. As

already defined, the basilisk is a fabulous animal with fiery death-dealing eyes and breath, so named from its crownlike crest.)

414 tragelaphus] In Greek mythology, a fabulous animal combining the form of a goat with that of a stag, or male deer.

414 leviathan] A huge and formidable aquatic beast, sometimes identified with the whale.

415 mantichoras] Manticore: in Greek mythology, a fabulous monster possessing the head of a man with horns, the body of a lion, and the tail or sting of a scorpion or a dragon, in addition to the quills or spines of a porcupine on the lion's body. (Now, there you have a truly composite beast!)

416 geryon] In Greek mythology, a winged monster with three bodies.

417 afrite] Afrit, afreet: in Arabic mythology, a powerful evil jinni, demon, or giant. (In the Islamic world, a jinni is one of a class of supernatural beings, sometimes subject to magic control.)

423 Rutilicus] Zeta Herculis, a fine binary or double star with a period or cycle of 34 years.

424 gyre] A ring, circle, or oval described by a moving object; also, an orbit described by a heavenly body.

432 Alioth] Word of Arabic origin: a star of the first or second magnitude in the handle of the Big Dipper, i.e., the seven principal stars in the constellation of Ursa Major.

435 scolopendras] Scolopendra: a Latin word meaning a kind of multiped, or animal having many feet. It would seem to mean, as used by Smith, an incredibly long and large monster with many legs—a macrocosmic centipede.

438 cockodrills] Cockodrill, cocodril: both obsolete forms or spellings for crocodile, from the French cocodrille; evidently, an incredibly large crocodile, or crocodilelike monster.

439 spleenful pygmies] Angry, spiteful, or malicious dwarfs.

440 Saiph] Word of Arabic origin for the star Kappa Orionis, i.e., in the constellation Orion (pronounced "safe" or "sa-eef" and meaning "sword"). Orion is known as Al-Jebbar, or the Giant, to the Arabs:

thus, the star serves as the sword for both the hunter Orion and the Giant. Saiph is a blue-white star intensely luminous and remote.

444   eidola] Eidolons, plural of eidolon: an image, idol, illusion, or phantom. All forms, whether singular or plural, are usually pronounced with the accent on the second syllable; however, they may also be pronounced with the accent on the first syllable. (Characteristically employed by Edgar Allan Poe in his poetry with the accent on the first syllable; Smith often follows Poe's usage exactly.)

448   abyss] Also as abysm: a bottomless or unfathomable depth or gulf. (Compare with *the Pit* in line 555.)

449   Demogorgons] Demogorgon: an enigmatic, terrifying, and evil god who commands the spirits of the lower or infernal world, and who appears in mediaeval literature as a demon of magic or as a primordial creative power. (Compare with the Demiurge of Platonic or Gnostic philosophy.)

466   irrespirable verge] Breathless edge, rim, brink. The point at which one's breath (temporarily) fails or stops because of the profound awe or fright induced by the inconceivable depth of descent beyond.

476   opal] 478 iris] Both words are used in the course of lines 470–90 in regard to objects that are multicolored or that exhibit a rainbowlike play of colors.

479   charnel] Derived from carnal, pertaining to meat or flesh. Of or like a charnel house: an edifice or chamber wherein are placed the bones or bodies of the dead: hence, pertaining to mortality or death.

495   carnelians] Carnelian: also derived from carnal, or Latin carneus. Fleshy, because of its color: a reddish-brown variety of clear chalcedony used as a gem.

497   rutilance] Here, reddishness, ruddiness, rubicundity, similar to rubescence or erubescence.

499   Kobold] In German folklore, an underground sprite associated with mines, quarries, etc., one of a group somewhat similar to gnomes.

520   the void] The empty space between the stars or the galaxies or beyond the cosmos; emptiness; nothingness.

534   occlusion] Here, obstruction: hence, darkness, obscurity.

538   ravin] Generally, death and destruction. Here, something seized and eaten as prey.

539   harpies] Harpy: in Greek mythology, one of a group of foul, malign creatures, half woman, half bird, that snatched away the souls of the dead, or seized or defiled the food of their victims.

544   embattled night and flame] As though the "foul, colossal Worms," rearing up, were pillars or columns compounded of night and fire, and thus "embattled," or prepared for battle.

546   wyvers] Wyver: a viper.

554   flaffing] Flaff: to flap or flutter.

555   the Pit] Hell: the bottomless pit. (Compare with *abyss* in line 448.)

557   torrent] Torrential: pertaining not only to an overwhelming rush or flow but here, specifically, burning, or emitting fire or flames.

568   convene] Gather, assemble.

The final image

The "huge white eyeless Face, / [. . .] / With lips of flame that open." In Smith's own words, this image is the symbol for infinity, thus a face that has no eyes (possibly indicating a lack of intelligence, or at least of absolute intelligence) but that does have flaming lips that open (possibly indicating either an almost mindless appetite or the preparation for some tremendous and ultimately awesome pronouncement). This image is perhaps also a manifestation or symbol of the Demiurge, as well as of an ultimate Demogorgon in its aspect or capacity as a (rather frightful) primordial creative power.

Suggested interpretation

What, then, is the meaning of this visual and emotional horror, this face *of* infinity, this face *from* infinity, this Demiurge, this Demogorgon? It is clearly much more than the fright induced, on the one hand, by some kind of colossal bug-eyed monster or, on the other hand, in this context, by some kind of macrocosmic monster without eyes. The meaning also involves even more than what is indicated by Smith's own theory or interpretation—the meaning actually subsumes his own theory—i.e., "that, if the infinite worlds of the cosmos were opened to human vision, the visionary would be overwhelmed by horror in the end, like the hero of this poem." It is the realization in emotional and then in intellectual terms—or at least the very strong fear or suspicion—that there is, at the centre of things, whether anywhere or everywhere, no ultimate and supremely intelligent God. This realization thus puts Smith and his overall output at the front line of the modernism of the twentieth century—or of any mere modernism of any historic period—and in the thick of the existential dilemma.

Conclusion

Such issues or questions have probably occupied or even obsessed certain intelligent and sensitive entities—including selected human individuals—if not from the beginning of time (at least as such a phrase involves sentient creatures living on our own planet), then from that time when our ancestors were first able to see beyond their most basic needs of survival, to look up at the night skies with its infinitude of eyes or stars staring back down at them, and to feel a sensation of awe, veneration, and solemn wonder at the cosmos in which they found themselves. And inasmuch as there will never be any kind of satisfying answer or adequate resolution to them, such issues or questions will continue to occupy and to obsess us until our species ceases to exist.

In the face of the often overwhelming awe, love and fear that we can feel when looking out into the cosmos from the vantage point of our own planet, we have evolved certain simple or complicated responses which have given rise to art, poetry, religion, philosophy, science, etc. Religion, philosophy, and science all embody attempts to dispel something of the ferocious fright, insecurity, and insignificance that we can feel when contemplating our little and rather impotent selves in relation to the enormousness of the cosmos and the ultimately unknown and unknowable powers or forces that permeate it. Knowing the immutable nature of humanity, religion at its best on occasion has not only afforded us much and much-needed comfort, but has also come up with considerable insight and wisdom in regard to humankind in relation to the cosmos, along with religion's often irrational articles of faith. On the other hand, like sophistication, science is the product of knowledge; but to pass from the ridiculous to the sublime, unlike sophistication, science is the creator of something like absolute knowledge of a certain limited class. However, in and of itself, by its very nature, science can have no wisdom, although it can supply us with marvellous and often incredible tools and insights. We supply the wisdom if we are fortunate enough to have it. Unfortunately, along with all the good things that they may have afforded us, religion and science have also produced other and negative effects. As Smith has himself observed (among his other apothegms and *pensées*), "Both religion and science, in their separate ways, have tried to destroy the inherent mystery of things by offering solutions. Fortunately, neither of them has succeeded; and mystery remains inviolate." Continuing in the same vein, he adds, and with more than usual perception, "To destroy wonder and mystery, is to destroy the only elements that make existence tolerable." So, despite our best efforts to the contrary, we shall end our own cycle as a species with what we began after all: the environing cosmos with its eternal wonder and mystery.

Printed in the United States
203293BV00004B/1-105/P